KIRK CAMERON
RAY COMFORT

CONQUER
YOUR FEAR
SHARE
YOUR
FAITH

Regal

From Gospel Light
Ventura, California, U.S.A.

D1708997

Published by Regal
From Gospel Light
Ventura, California, U.S.A.
www.regalbooks.com
Printed in the U.S.A.

All Scripture quotations, unless otherwise indicated, are taken from the *New King James Version*.
Copyright © 1979, 1980, 1982 by Thomas Nelson, Inc. Used by permission. All rights reserved.

Other version used is *King James Version*. Authorized King James Version.

© 2009 Ray Comfort and Kirk Cameron
All rights reserved.

All photos in the book by Carol Scott, CJ-Studio.com, Covina, California. Used by permission.

Library of Congress Cataloging-in-Publication Data
Comfort, Ray.
Conquer your fear, share your faith : leader's guide / Ray Comfort and Kirk Cameron.
p. cm.
ISBN 978-0-8307-5152-5 (trade paper)
1. Witness bearing (Christianity)—Study and teaching. I. Cameron, Kirk, 1970- II. Title.
BV4520.C6343 2009
269'.2071—dc22
2009010299

Rights for publishing this book outside the U.S.A. or in non-English languages are
administered by Gospel Light Worldwide, an international not-for-profit ministry.
For additional information, please visit www.glww.org, email info@glww.org, or write to
Gospel Light Worldwide, 1957 Eastman Avenue, Ventura, CA 93003, U.S.A.

CONTENTS

Leading the Course

Q & A

Additional Materials

INTRODUCTION

Welcome to *Conquer Your Fear, Share Your Faith* training course! We hope that this will be the most powerful, eye-opening evangelism experience for you and for those who go through this course with you.

Perhaps you have tried different evangelism programs and become discouraged or disillusioned by people's responses. Like countless others through the ages, you will find, as we have, that using these *biblical* principles will revolutionize your life and witness. This is not some new method we have devised; it is a timeless truth firmly rooted in the pages of Scripture, validated by centuries of Church use and proven by our own practice for 20-plus years.

Evangelism is like swimming. You can talk about it until you are blue in the face, but if you don't dive in and do it, you will never swim. This course is all about diving in.

Do you remember the first time you drove a car? It probably seemed as if you had to remember to do a dozen things all at once. Steer straight. Watch the yellow line. Watch the rearview mirror. Keep your foot near the brake. Be ready to brake. Watch for other cars. Be on the lookout for pedestrians. Watch for cyclists who may swerve. Keep an eye on your speed. Watch for the law. Don't tailgate. But after driving for a while, you probably found that you could almost do these things blindfolded.

The same principles apply to evangelism. The first time you approach a stranger, you will be terrified. There are so many things to remember. Be ready to stop and listen. Use the Law. Watch for distractions. Head for the cross. But after you do it again and again, your confidence will grow and you will learn to steer the conversation anywhere you want. And if you will let love be your driving force, before you know it, evangelism will become a way of life.

Of course, you will have to battle your fears continually to do it, but once you step out and witness, you will be so confident that no atheist, evolutionist, intellectual, agnostic, Gnostic or even caustic person will intimidate you. Your only problem will be overconfidence. You will have to keep your heart free from pride, because that will hinder you, and you can't afford any hindrances when it comes to reaching out to the lost.

We have designed this Leader's Guide to help you lead a group through this course, using both the *Conquer Your Fear, Share Your Faith* DVD (in the back of this guide) and the *Conquer Your Fear, Share Your Faith* book. We encourage you to buy one copy of the *Conquer Your Fear, Share Your Faith* book for each of your group members, as it is a powerful primer on evangelism that goes deeper into each of the topics that we will address during the course.

This course has been designed so that you can conduct it in one of two ways: (1) as a one-day event, in which you teach all four sessions in a single day; or (2) as a four-week group course, in which you study one session a week, meeting once a week. In this guide, we will provide you with a schedule for each study option.

As you lead others through this course, we pray that you will get the tools and the courage you need to become an active and effective soul-winner in the harvest field. Whether you are already extensively involved in the Great Commission or desiring a deeper commitment, we pray that the Lord will give you a greater love for sinners and an urgency for lost souls today.

Thank you for the investment you are making in the lives of others to help further the kingdom of God.

God bless you,
Ray Comfort and Kirk Cameron

PREPARING TO LEAD THE COURSE

GETTING STARTED

This section will give you an overview of the materials and preparation needed to lead this course successfully.

Qualifications for Leading

A vital first step in successful evangelism training is to make sure that you understand and are practicing the principles of biblical evangelism given in this course. If you aren't well versed in its concepts, go through the course on your own first to be sure you're well grounded in its principles and prepared to answer any questions that attendees may ask. Most important, be sure you've actually put these principles into practice in witnessing so that you know first-hand their powerful impact in reaching the lost. Your testimony of its effectiveness and your enthusiasm for this teaching will be infectious and encouraging to others.

Once you're familiar with the *Conquer Your Fear, Share Your Faith* Evangelism Crash Course, facilitating the course doesn't require any special training—just a love for the Lord and for the lost. If you can simply follow the four-session outline in the "Leading the Course" section, provide a few materials to participants, get a copy of the *Conquer Your Fear, Share Your Faith* book for each participant and plan a "fishing trip" where you demonstrate these principles in witnessing, you are well qualified! Maintain a positive, prayerful attitude and expect God to do great things through your group.

Promoting the Course

It is recommended that you first go through this course with a smaller group within your church or a home study group. Once you're familiar with how to present the material and answer questions, we strongly urge you to continue assembling fresh, new groups to go through the course. As more "fishers of men" are faithful to put this teaching into practice, their excitement will be contagious and will attract additional people to take the training.

As we stated in the introduction, there are two ways you can conduct this course. In this guide, we have provided you with suggested schedules for doing this training as a four-week group study, or as a one-day event. If you choose to break the sessions up differently, simply adapt the schedules to best fit your needs for the group.

Regardless of the approach you employ, you will want to promote this course to those in other churches and to people in the community. Here are some ideas for how to do this:

- **Churches:** Provide bulletin inserts, flyers, posters and details to announce your one-day session or multiple group sessions. Posters can be hung in classrooms and around the church; flyers can be placed in a welcome center or given to youth leaders or Sunday School teachers to hand out in class (sample inserts, flyers and posters are included in pdf format on the accompanying DVD). The church may want to print a brief announcement in the bulletin or include an announcement in their newsletter or on their website. Whichever method they prefer, request that they promote the training session(s) for at least two consecutive weeks. Ask your pastor to announce the course from the pulpit and encourage people to attend (this carries much more weight than just listing the course in the bulletin). In addition, try to speak to the outreach pastor, youth pastor or leader and children's workers, inviting them to discover a vital principle that leads to genuine conversions.

- **Radio stations:** If you are planning on doing this course as a one-day event, advertising it on the radio could drastically increase your attendance. Provide details for the radio station's website community calendar (they may also want to announce events on the radio).

- **Newspapers:** You can also provide details to newspapers for their religion or community event sections. If you have a large event involving several churches, submit a brief news release and invite the newspaper to interview you.

- **Christian bookstores:** Place flyers or bulletin inserts on the counter, or provide a poster for a bulletin board. (The smaller bulletin insert is more likely to be given precious counter space.) You could also try milling around the store, handing customers a flyer and encouraging them to attend the course.

- **Home-school groups:** Provide details for their newsletter and website.

- **Christian groups in your area:** AWANA, Upward Basketball, FCA, Boy Scouts, Youth for Christ, the local YMCA and other organizations who work with children and youth may be interested in learning an effective way to share the gospel with those with whom they minister.

- **Previous attendees:** If you are planning other future courses, have a flyer ready to give to attendees at the end of the current course. Send email announcements to notify them of upcoming training opportunities so they can enthusiastically promote the course to others in their spheres of influence.

Like-minded individuals from other churches can approach their pastor or church staff to ask that they help promote the course. Once they get permission, it's best if the individual volunteers do the legwork (make copies, put up posters, announce to Sunday School classes). An individual who is passionate about the teaching will usually be more creative and thorough in promoting the event than a staff person.

If you don't know individuals in other churches, ask to speak with an appropriate pastor or staff member of those churches to share your enthusiasm for this life-changing—and eternity changing—training course. Explain how this material will help them greatly impact their church and community with the gospel.

To help you promote future courses, create a checklist of the various media with their contact information. That way, you can easily keep track of contact names for publicizing each event.

Needed Materials

As you prepare your materials and equipment, decide how you will cover the cost of materials and snacks for the class. People tend to take more ownership and interest in a class if they have some investment in it, however small that investment might be, but make sure that finances are not an obstacle to anyone who wants to attend.

To know how much material to order, publicize the course at least three weeks ahead of time and ask for a sign-up deadline one week before training begins. That should give you an approximate number of attendees, but be sure to order plenty of additional materials, as there will always be those people who sign up late. Here are some of the additional materials that you might need:

- **Sufficient tracts for each person.** We recommend that you order at least one pack each of the Way of the Master tracts to distribute some to each participant (available at www.WayoftheMaster.com). Tracts are an incredible icebreaker to help begin conversations, and they provide a great first step to help encourage people to get out of their comfort zone and share their faith.

- **Books for further study.** After discovering this teaching, most people are interested in more information about it, so we recommend that you set up a resource table where participants can purchase items at the end of the course. After you purchase a copy of the *Conquer Your Fear, Share Your Faith* book for every group member, consider providing other helpful evangelism books (such as *Way of the Master* or *Thanks a Million!*) and resources for your group. More books and resources can be purchased at www.WayoftheMaster.com or www.gospellight.com.

- **Quick Reference Card.** A quick reference card is included for participants on page 165 of this guide. A color, laminated version is also available for purchase from www.WayoftheMaster.com. The card can easily fit into a participant's pocket or purse and serves as a quick reference that he or she can glance at before witnessing to someone.

If anyone cannot afford a *Conquer Your Fear, Share Your Faith* book, or the Way of the Master tracts, you may want to offer them free of charge so no one misses out because of lack of finances. Depending on your funds, you may also want to purchase an optional video clip resource such as "Eight Reasons Why I Don't Share My Faith," which you can show at the beginning of the course. (To preview this video clip, go to www.WayoftheMaster.com/crash course.) We find that it is a wonderful tool for helping participants laugh at themselves as they recognize the fears we all have about sharing our faith.

Materials at a Glance

- *Conquer Your Fear, Share Your Faith* (order one book for each person)
- **Tracts** (order several for each person)
- *The Way of the Master* book (*suggested*)
- *Thanks a Million!* book (*suggested*)
- **Quick Reference Card** (*suggested*)
- **"Eight Reasons Why I Don't Share My Faith" video clip** (*suggested*)

Make copies of the sign-in sheet (see page 21). For a complete checklist of items you will need for the course, see page 23.

Fishing Trip

The goal of this course is not simply to have people watch the material but also to transform them into confident witnesses for Jesus Christ. We must be *doers* of the Word, and not hearers only (see James 1:22). Jesus called us to be fishers of men (see Mark 1:17). Therefore, after going through entire course, invite participants to join you for regular times of witnessing at a local "fishing hole." Once they see these principles in action, they will discover how easy it is to approach people and share the gospel in a friendly, non-confrontational way. At first, participants won't be expected to say anything at this time—just observe—so encourage all of them to come and learn.

Of course, depending on the "fear factor" of your group, you may *choose* to ask them to participate. Whatever their experience level in witnessing, encourage them to take at least one step out of their comfort zone today. By overcoming their fears, they will discover the exhilaration that comes from obeying the Lord and being used to impact a person's eternity.

After session four of this course, you will also have the option of taking your group on a "fishing trip" to try out what they've learned. Select a location for this fishing trip and make any necessary arrangements. Choose a place where lots of "fish" gather, such as an outdoor shopping center, a movie theater, a coffee house, an ice cream store and so on. Make sure it is on public property. Plan to have a quick meal (for example, order pizza in advance) and have a time of prayer before you go out. To make sure there is plenty of time for conversations, allocate a couple of hours for witnessing.

It is important to also plan a short time to meet at the end of the evening for a quick celebration and "debriefing." Discussing your successes and failures will energize participants and encourage everyone present. Give praises to God for the glorious gospel—and for giving everyone the boldness to come to this event! Be sure to also pray for those who listened to the gospel.

Reminder Email

A few days before the class, email or call those who have signed up to remind them of the date, schedule and location. With so much material to cover, ask them to be on time so that the class can start promptly. To avoid scaring the "fish" away on the outing after class, encourage participants not to dress in any "witness wear" that clearly identifies them as Christians.

TIPS FOR SUCCESS

The following recommendations will help you create a strong foundation for an effective learning environment in your group meetings.

Eliminate Distractions

After watching the life-changing videos on the DVD included at the back of this Leader's Guide, one man confessed that he had been entertaining sin and, with tears streaming down his face, cried out to God in front of the whole class. Some people, after watching the "True & False Conversions" video in session three, have openly confessed that they didn't think they were saved. Others have said they couldn't sleep that night because the Lord was dealing with them so heavily.

Because these videos are so powerful and cover a lot of crucial material in a short amount of time, it's important to watch them without any interruptions. Make every effort to keep people's attention from being diverted. The following suggestions can help you remove distractions from the learning environment:

- **Room arrangement**: Arrange chairs so participants are facing away from the door.

- **Tables**: If you're holding the course in a larger venue, place registration and refreshment tables at the back of the room near the door.

- **Resources**: If you are making other resources available, place them on a table away from the entrance and don't mention them until the end of the class. You may want to place a sheet over the table to limit curiosity.

- **Children**: Firmly insist on not allowing young children in the class, as it will be difficult for them to sit quietly through the entire session without fidgeting or being disruptive. If childcare isn't an available option, you may want to consider holding a private training course in a home for parents of young kids.

Provide Refreshments

It is a good idea to provide refreshments for the participants. Set the drinks out first, and as people come in, direct them to the refreshment table and invite them to help themselves to something to drink. If you are doing this course over four meetings, you may want to wait until the end of the meeting to set out snacks (such as cookies); if you are doing this as a one-day event, you can set out snacks during the first break. Participants will have been sitting for a while, and a treat may help refresh them and keep them alert. In addition, if you are doing this as a one-day event, you will also want to order lunch to serve to participants during the break time.

Make It a Team Effort

It is recommended that you invite others to help you in preparing and presenting the course. Here are three ways to do this:

- **Set-up**: Ask others to help gather materials and set up the room. They can provide snacks and drinks, bring the paper products, handle registration, man the resource table, and so forth.

- **Q&A**: If other people are familiar with this teaching, have one or two help you handle the question and answer time. Different personalities will resonate with different people, so having multiple people answer questions can be advantageous. Just make sure the people you invite are trusted individuals in whom you have full confidence.

- **Optional Testimonies**: If possible, have a couple of seasoned fishermen come up after each break to give a very brief testimony. This could include an account of a divine appointment, how they struggled to overcome fear, a demonstration of ways to start conversations, and so on—whatever the Lord leads them to say. Hearing from a variety of people will encourage participants that they can do this as well.

For any helpers who have already seen the videos on the DVD, remind them before class to not talk or get up during the sessions. They need to give their full attention to the teaching to show others the importance of the videos and to better enable them to answer any questions about the content.

Fan the Flame

The goal of this material is to train up laborers who will go out into the harvest field on a regular basis. To help make evangelism truly a lifestyle, strongly encourage participants to do the following:

- **Ask a friend to join them and go out together to "fish for men."** This could occur at various impromptu times or on a regular PIE night (prayer, intercession and evangelism), where they grab a bite to eat, pray together, and then hit the streets or a mall to seek the lost. Whatever they do—handing out tracts, doing one-to-one witnessing or open-air preaching—make sure they do *something* to continue reaching out to their families, friends, neighbors, coworkers and the strangers they encounter throughout they week. The participant and his or her friend can share witnessing experiences and encourage one another to "abound still more and more" (Philippians 1:9) in the work of the Lord.

- **Continue their training to become further equipped.** Whether alone, in pairs or as a group, those who so desire can get additional training in this type of evangelism by watching "The Way of the Master" episodes, viewing the online videos going through the eight-week DVD studies (Basic and Intermediate Training Courses) available at www.livingwaters.com, or enrolling in the School of Biblical Evangelism (see www.biblicalevangelism.com), and so on. In this way they can keep fanning the flame sparked by this course so that the fire will never go out.

If possible, begin meeting regularly for this purpose after completing the *Conquer Your Fear, Share Your Faith* Evangelism Crash Course, and invite all attendees to continue to participate.

COURSE SIGN-IN SHEET

Name	Phone	Email Address
_____	_____	_____
_____	_____	_____
_____	_____	_____
_____	_____	_____
_____	_____	_____
_____	_____	_____
_____	_____	_____
_____	_____	_____
_____	_____	_____
_____	_____	_____
_____	_____	_____
_____	_____	_____
_____	_____	_____
_____	_____	_____
_____	_____	_____
_____	_____	_____
_____	_____	_____
_____	_____	_____
_____	_____	_____

© 2009 Kirk Cameron and Ray Comfort. Permission to photocopy granted.

COURSE CHECKLIST

- ❏ Television and DVD player (test before class to be sure they're working)
- ❏ *Conquer Your Fear* DVD (including in this Leader's Guide)
- ❏ *Conquer Your Fear, Share Your Faith* books
- ❏ Area for sign-in and course materials, refreshments and resources
- ❏ Extra pens or pencils
- ❏ Sign-in sheet
- ❏ Nametags and markers
- ❏ Snacks
- ❏ Drinks
- ❏ Napkins
- ❏ Cups
- ❏ *The Way of the Master* books (suggested)
- ❏ *Thanks a Million!* and *What Did Jesus Do?* books (suggested)
- ❏ Tracts (suggested)
- ❏ Sheet to cover resource area until end of class (suggested)
- ❏ Maps showing how to get to the "fishing hole"
- ❏ Flyer for the next class (if available)

© 2009 Kirk Cameron and Ray Comfort. Permission to photocopy granted.

SAMPLE ANNOUNCEMENTS

SAMPLE
ONE-DAY EVENT PULPIT ANNOUNCEMENT

Would you invest a few hours . . . to impact someone's eternity? Most Christians don't share their faith because they don't feel equipped. The *Conquer Your Fear, Share Your Faith* course with Kirk Cameron and Ray Comfort will change all that. You can learn to share your faith simply and effectively here on Saturday, August 12, 8:00 A.M.–12:30 P.M., at Grace of God Church.

In four powerful, eye-opening videos, Kirk and Ray will give you the confidence and the tools you need to share your faith with anyone. At the end of this FREE class, you will be invited to go out and see these principles put into practice in real-life witnessing. Lunch will be provided.

Registration for the class ends August 5, so sign up today. For more information, call Joe Smith at 555-1212.

SAMPLE
FOUR-WEEK GROUP COURSE PULPIT ANNOUNCEMENT

Would you invest a few hours . . . to impact someone's eternity? Most Christians don't share their faith because they don't feel equipped. The *Conquer Your Fear, Share Your Faith* course featuring Kirk Cameron and Ray Comfort will change that! You can learn to share your faith simply and effectively in four weekly sessions held at the Smith's home on Thursday nights from August 5 to August 26. The session will begin at 7:30 P.M. and end around 9:00 P.M.

In four powerful, eye-opening videos, Ray Comfort and Kirk Cameron will give you the confidence and the tools you need to share your faith with anyone. At the end of this FREE class, you will be invited to go out and see these principles put into practice in real-life witnessing. Refreshments provided!

To sign up for the class, please contact Joe Smith at 555-1212 by August 1.

CONQUER YOUR FEAR, SHARE YOUR FAITH

Do you want to want to share your faith with others, but don't know where to start? Are you paralyzed with fear at the prospects of sharing the gospel with a complete stranger? Have you tried evangelism programs but become discouraged by people's responses? If so, the one-day *Conquer Your Fear, Share Your Faith* course is for you!

Learn to share your faith simply and effectively in four powerful, eye-opening sessions featuring DVD presentations hosted by Kirk Cameron and Ray Comfort.

Cost: FREE
When: Saturday, Aug. 15, 8:00 a.m. – 12:30 p.m.
Where: Grace of God Church, 1800 Rose Rd.
Register by: August 5

After class, come and watch real-life witnessing.
Lunch is provided!

FOR MORE INFORMATION, CALL:
Joe Smith at 555-1212

Invest a few hours . . .
and learn to impact eternity.

Note: This announcement is available in PDF format on the *Conquer Your Fear, Share Your Faith* DVD.

CONQUER YOUR FEAR, SHARE YOUR FAITH

Do you want to want to share your faith with others, but don't know where to start? Are you paralyzed with fear at the prospects of sharing the gospel with a complete stranger? Have you tried evangelism programs but become discouraged by people's responses? If so, the *Conquer Your Fear, Share Your Faith* course is for you!

In four weekly sessions, featuring powerful, eye-opening DVDs hosted by Kirk Cameron and Ray Comfort, you will learn how to share your faith simply and effectively.

Cost: FREE
When: Thursday nights, Aug 5-26, 7:30-9:00 p.m.
Where: The Smith's home, 1800 Washington Rd.
Please RSVP by: August 1

Following the sessions, you will have the opportunity to come and watch real-life witnessing on Sat, August 29

FOR MORE INFORMATION, CALL:
Joe Smith at 555-1212

Invest a few hours . . .
and learn to impact eternity.

Note: This announcement is available in PDF format on the *Conquer Your Fear, Share Your Faith* DVD.

SAMPLE
ONE-DAY EVENT FLYER

WHO DO YOU KNOW WHO ISN'T SAVED?

WHAT ARE YOU DOING TO REACH THEM?

Would you invest a few hours . . . to learn to impact eternity?

When:

Saturday, Aug. 15, 8:00 a.m. – 12:30 p.m.

Learn to share your faith with family, friends and strangers in the *Conquer Your Fear, Share Your Faith* course!

In four sessions, featuring powerful, eye-opening DVDs hosted by Kirk Cameron and Ray Comfort, you will learn how to share your faith simply and effectively.

FREE Class!

Where: Grace of God Church, 1800 Rose Rd.

Register by: August 5

TO REGISTER OR FOR MORE INFORMATION, CALL:

Joe Smith at 555-1212

Note: This flyer is available in PDF format on the *Conquer Your Fear, Share Your Faith* DVD.

SAMPLE
FOUR-WEEK GROUP COURSE FLYER

WHO DO YOU KNOW WHO ISN'T SAVED?

WHAT ARE YOU DOING TO REACH THEM?

Do you want to want to share your faith with others, but don't know where to start? Are you paralyzed with fear at the prospects of sharing the gospel with a complete stranger? Have you tried evangelism programs but become discouraged by people's responses? If so, the *Conquer Your Fear, Share Your Faith* course is for you!

In four weekly sessions, featuring powerful, eye-opening DVDs hosted by Kirk Cameron and Ray Comfort, you will learn how to share your faith simply and effectively.

Cost: FREE
When: Thursday nights, Aug 5-26, 7:30-9:00 p.m.
Where: The Smith's home, 1800 Washington Rd.
Please RSVP by: August 1

Following the sessions, you will have the opportunity to come and watch real-life witnessing on Sat, August 29

FOR MORE INFORMATION, CALL:
Joe Smith at 555-1212

Invest a few hours . . .
and learn to impact eternity.

Note: This flyer is available in PDF format on the *Conquer Your Fear, Share Your Faith* DVD.

SAMPLE

ONE-DAY EVENT POSTER

WHO DO YOU KNOW WHO ISN'T SAVED?
WHAT ARE YOU DOING TO REACH THEM?

Would you invest a few hours . . . to learn to impact eternity?

When:

Saturday, Aug. 15, 8:00 a.m. - 12:30 p.m.

Learn to share your faith with family, friends and strangers in the *Conquer Your Fear, Share Your Faith* course!

In four sessions, featuring powerful, eye-opening DVDs hosted by Kirk Cameron and Ray Comfort, you will learn how to share your faith simply and effectively.

FREE Class!

Where: Grace of God Church, 1800 Rose Rd.

Register by: August 5

TO REGISTER OR FOR MORE INFORMATION, CALL:

Joe Smith at 555-1212

THE WAY OF THE MASTER

has been endorsed by John MacArthur, Josh McDowell, D. James Kennedy, Ravi Zacharias, Charles Stanley, Franklin Graham, Lee Strobel, George Barna and many others.

Note: This poster is available in PDF format on the *Conquer Your Fear, Share Your Faith* DVD.

WHO DO YOU KNOW WHO ISN'T SAVED?

WHAT ARE YOU DOING TO REACH THEM?

Would you invest a few hours . . . to learn to impact eternity?

Learn to share your faith with family, friends and strangers in the *Conquer Your Fear, Share Your Faith* course!

In four weekly sessions, featuring powerful, eye-opening DVDs hosted by Kirk Cameron and Ray Comfort, you will learn how to share your faith simply and effectively.

FREE Class!

When: Thursday nights, Aug 5-26, 7:30-9:00 p.m.

Where: The Smith's home, 1800 Washington Rd.

Please RSVP by: August 1

FOR MORE INFORMATION, CALL:

Joe Smith at 555-1212

THE WAY OF THE MASTER

has been endorsed by
John MacArthur, Josh McDowell,
D. James Kennedy, Ravi Zacharias,
Charles Stanley, Franklin Graham,
Lee Strobel, George Barna
and many others.

Note: This poster is available in PDF format on the *Conquer Your Fear, Share Your Faith* DVD.

LEADING
THE COURSE

BEFORE YOU BEGIN

As we mentioned in the introduction, before the first session begins, make sure that each participant has a copy of the *Conquer Your Fear, Share Your Faith* book. If you are conducting the course as a one-day event, you can have participants pick up the book when they sign up or register for the course. If you are doing this over the course of four weeks, you can either hand the materials out to group members prior to the first meeting or set aside some time before session one for the participants get their books. It is important in either case to have participants complete "The Love Test" before you go into session one, as this will provide them with an overview of where they stand on sharing their faith.

When the participants arrive, ask them to fill out the sign-in sheet (see page 21). Be sure to explain to them that their phone number and email address will be shared with other attendees so they can contact one another. Announce where the restrooms are located and suggest that they take advantage of the opportunity now so that they can remain seated during the video presentations. Ask everyone to silence his or her cell phone during the sessions (and no texting!).

On the following pages is a copy of "The Love Test" (which is also included in the Student Guide in the back of the *Conquer Your Fear, Share Your Faith* book) and two course schedule options. The first schedule (see pages 42-44) is a suggested timeline for completing this course as a one-day event; the second schedule (see pages 45-48) is a suggested timeline for completing the course in four individual weekly group sessions. Outlines for each of the sessions in the *Conquer Your Fear, Share Your Faith* course can also be found on pages 49-79.

THE LOVE TEST

Take this test before the first video teaching. With an honest heart, contemplate these statements.

1. The thought of sharing my faith:
   a. Terrifies me
   b. Embarrasses me
   c. Excites me
   d. Bores me

2. I believe the person with whom I share my faith would probably:
   a. Thank me
   b. Physically attack me
   c. Think I'm a fanatic
   d. It doesn't matter what they do to me

3. If I saw a blind man walking toward a 1,000-foot cliff, I would immediately:
   a. Offer him my favorite Christian CD
   b. Invite him to my house for a non-confrontational BBQ the following weekend
   c. Suggest a more fulfilling place to walk
   d. Warn him about the cliff

4. The fact that anyone could suffer in hell forever:
   a. Doesn't worry me
   b. Concerns me
   c. Horrifies me
   d. Isn't my problem

5. I could conquer my fears about sharing my faith if each time I tried I was given:
   a. $20
   b. $100
   c. $1,000
   d. A promise that God would be with me

6. According to Colossians 1:28, we are told that we should be warning:
   a. All Jews
   b. Our relatives
   c. Every person
   d. Every Christian

7. In light of that command, I have been:

   a. Disobedient
   b. Faithful
   c. Unaware of my responsibility
   d. Complacent

8. I am:

   a. An on-fire Christian who will use any possible way to reach the lost with the gospel
   b. Neither hot nor cold, but lukewarm (see Revelation 3:16)
   c. Not sure if my love for Christ is strong enough (see John 14:15)

9. A person who is not born again will:

   a. Be eternally happy
   b. Die unfulfilled
   c. Still go to heaven
   d. Spend eternity in hell

10. When Paul pleaded with the people on Mars Hill (Acts 17), he demonstrated his concern for them by:

   a. Inviting them to a worship service in the upper room
   b. Smiling and hoping they noticed the peace in his eyes
   c. Saying something to make them feel good about themselves
   d. Telling them about the coming Day of Judgment and what they must do to be saved

11. If we know someone who is not born again, we should do all we can to:

   a. Spend months building their trust and hope they ask us what makes us different (assuming they don't die first...which we can't assume)
   b. Invite them to church and hope they want to come back
   c. Wear a cross around our neck so they'll know we're sold out for Jesus
   d. Learn to go to them in love and compassion, speaking the truth, leading them to the Savior

12. In light of the fact that 150,000 people die every day, and I know how to cure death, what would I like to do now?

   a. Pray about it
   b. Leave this training session before it even gets started
   c. Begin to learn how to share my faith, effectively, biblically—the way Jesus did—and reach the lost with the gospel

SAMPLE COURSE SCHEDULES

One-Day Event Schedule

BEFORE THE COURSE BEGINS		
ACTIVITY	**TIME**	**DESCRIPTION**
Registration/ Check-in	N/A	Have participants sign in at one of the tables in the back of your meeting place. Instruct them to pick up a copy of the *Conquer Your Fear, Share Your Faith* book and complete "The Love Test" before the session begins.
SESSION 1: THE FIREFIGHTER		
Welcome/ Prayer	3 min.	Welcome participants, give an overview of the course, and open the course in prayer.
Introduction	2 min.	Briefly share a little about yourself and why you're leading this course.
Icebreaker	10-15 min.	Have each participant share his or her name and why he or she is attending this course.
Session 1 DVD	26 min.	Introduce and show session 1, "The Firefighter," and have participants take notes in the *Conquer Your Fear, Share Your Faith* Student Guide.
Break/Quiz	15 min.	Have participants complete the session 1 quiz in the Student Guide and pick up refreshments at the back table.
Q&A	3 min.	Answer any questions and hand out copies of the Q&A section from the Leader's Guide, if needed.
SESSION 2: HELL'S BEST KEPT SECRET		
Testimonials	6-10 min.	Share a story of your own evangelism experience and how you overcame your fear, or have one or two other trusted evangelists share their experiences.

Session 2 DVD	34 min.	Introduce and show session 2, "Hell's Best Kept Secret," and have participants take notes in the *Conquer Your Fear, Share Your Faith* Student Guide.
Break/Quiz	20 min.	Have participants complete the session 2 quiz in their *Conquer Your Fear, Share Your Faith* Student Guide, and then read the quiz answers aloud to the group. Invite participants to pick up refreshments at the back table.
Discussion Time	10-12 min.	Ask the two questions provided in this Leader's Guide and have participants break into small groups of 3 to 5 people to discuss. Share their answers with the larger group.
Q&A	3 min.	Answer any questions and hand out copies of the Q&A section from the Leader's Guide, if needed.
Lunch Break	30-45 min.	Take a lunch break before finishing the final two sessions.

SESSION 3: TRUE & FALSE CONVERSIONS

Session 3 DVD	26 min.	Introduce and show session 3, "True & False Conversions," and have participants take notes in the *Conquer Your Fear, Share Your Faith* Student Guide.
Break/Quiz	20 min.	Have participants complete the session 3 quiz in their *Conquer Your Fear, Share Your Faith* Student Guide, and then read the quiz answers aloud to the group. Invite participants to pick up refreshments at the back table.
Discussion Time	10-12 min.	Ask the two questions provided in this Leader's Guide and have participants break into small groups of 3 to 5 people to discuss. Share their answers with the larger group.
Q&A	3 min.	Answer any questions and hand out copies of the Q&A section from the Leader's Guide, if needed.

SESSION 4: WHAT DID JESUS DO?

Session 4 DVD	36 min.	Introduce and show session 4, "What Did Jesus Do," and have participants take notes in the *Conquer Your Fear, Share Your Faith* Student Guide.
Break/Quiz	15 min.	Have participants complete the session 4 quiz in the Student Guide and pick up refreshments at the back table.
Demonstration of Tracts/ Role-Playing	20 min.	Have the participants break off into pairs to do the role-playing exercise. (You might want to demonstrate this activity up front with a participant or coleader before the participants break into pairs.)
Homework/ Closing Prayer	5 min.	Offer any closing remarks for the course, and then conclude by encouraging students to read their *Conquer Your Fear, Share Your Faith* books for further instruction. Pray for the participants as they prepare to go out and share their faith.

OPTIONAL: FISHING TRIP

Fishing Trip	1-3 hrs.	Give participants the opportunity to go out with you and other trusted fishing partners to see these principles put into practice.

Four-Week Group Course Schedule

SESSION 1: THE FIREFIGHTER

ACTIVITY	TIME	DESCRIPTION
Pre-session	N/A	Greet participants and have them pick up a copy of the *Conquer Your Fear, Share Your Faith* book (this could happen at any time before the first session begins). Instruct them to complete "The Love Test" before the session starts.
Welcome/ Prayer	3 min.	Welcome participants, give an overview of the course, and open the course in prayer.
Introduction	2 min.	Briefly share a little about yourself and why you are leading this course.
Icebreaker	10-15 min.	Have each participant share why he or she is attending this course.
Session 1 DVD	30 min.	Introduce the session 1 DVD and read through the "Three Minutes to Live" script. Show session 1, "The Firefighter," and have participants take notes in the *Conquer Your Fear, Share Your Faith* Student Guide.
Break/Quiz	15 min.	Allow students to take a quick break, and then have them complete the session 1 quiz in the Student Guide.
Discussion Time	5 min.	If the group is large, have participants break into small groups of 3 to 5 people to discuss the quiz answers.
Q&A/ Homework	3-5 min.	Answer any questions and hand out copies of the Q&A section from the Leader's Guide, if needed. Briefly mention the homework for next week.

SESSION 2: HELL'S BEST KEPT SECRET

Welcome/ Prayer	3 min.	Welcome participants, give an overview of the second session, and ask God to lead your time together.
Testimonials	6-10 min.	Share a story of your own evangelism experience and how you overcame your fear, or have one or two other trusted evangelists share their experiences.
Session 2 DVD	34 min.	Introduce and show session 2, "Hell's Best Kept Secret," and have participants take notes in the *Conquer Your Fear, Share Your Faith* Student Guide.
Break/Quiz	20 min.	Allow students to take a quick break, and then have them complete the session 2 quiz in the Student Guide. Read the quiz answers aloud to the group.
Discussion Time	10-12 min.	Ask the two questions provided in this Leader's Guide and, if the group is large, have participants break into small groups of 3 to 5 people to discuss. Share their answers with the larger group.
Q&A / Homework	3-5 min.	Answer any questions and hand out copies of the Q&A section from the Leader's Guide, if needed. Briefly mention the homework for next.

SESSION 3: TRUE & FALSE CONVERSIONS

Welcome/ Prayer	3 min.	Welcome participants, give an overview of the third session, and ask God to lead your time together.
Session 3 DVD	26 min.	Introduce and show session 3, "True & False Conversions," and have participants take notes in the *Conquer Your Fear, Share Your Faith* Student Guide.
Break/Quiz	20 min.	Allow students to take a quick break, and then have them complete the session 3 quiz in the Student Guide. Read the quiz answers aloud to the group.
Discussion Time	10-12 min.	Ask the two questions provided in this Leader's Guide and, if the group is large, have participants break into small groups of 3 to 5 people to discuss. Share their answers with the larger group.
Q&A / Homework	3-5 min.	Answer any questions and hand out copies of the Q&A section from the Leader's Guide, if needed. Briefly mention the homework for next week.

SESSION 4: WHAT DID JESUS DO?

Welcome/ Prayer	3 min.	Welcome participants, give an overview of the fourth session, and ask God to lead your time together.
Session 4 DVD	36 min.	Introduce and show session 4, "What Did Jesus Do," and have participants take notes in the *Conquer Your Fear, Share Your Faith* Student Guide.
Break/Quiz	15 min.	Allow students to take a quick break, and then have them complete the session 4 quiz in the Student Guide.
Demonstration of Tracts/ Role-Playing	20 min.	Have the participants break off into pairs to do the role-playing exercise. (You might want to demonstrate this activity up front with a participant or coleader before the participants break into pairs.)
Closing Remarks	7-10 min.	Conclude the course and encourage students to continue reading their *Conquer Your Fear, Share Your Faith* books. Pray for the participants as they prepare to go out and share their faith.

OPTIONAL: FISHING TRIP

Fishing Trip	1-3 hrs.	Give participants the opportunity to go out with you and other trusted fishing partners to see these principles put into practice.

SESSION

1

THE FIREFIGHTER

Welcome/Prayer

Welcome participants to the training course and thank them for giving of their time to become an effective witness for our Lord. There is no greater joy than to be used by the Lord to seek and save the lost. Then pray, asking God to give you a deeper understanding of evangelism and a genuine concern for the lost.

Course Introduction

Begin the class by introducing yourself, briefly sharing a little about yourself and why you're leading this course. If there are experienced fishermen in the class who are helping you, introduce those individuals and thank them for coming to support and equip others. Let the class know how invaluable these people are and that they are there to encourage them and answer any questions they have.

Icebreaker

As time allows, go around the room and have each participant give their name and *briefly* share why they have come to this class. What are they hoping to accomplish by taking this course? What are their biggest concerns, frustrations or fears when it comes to sharing their faith? Don't hesitate to remind people to keep it brief (approximately one minute) and don't allow questions at this point. If there are questions, you can assure them that any concerns will be addressed during the course or the Q&A time.

"The Firefighter" DVD

Explain that the Student Guide for the course is in the back of the *Conquer Your Fear, Share Your Faith* book (you can also provide participants with a copy of the student handouts found in this guide). Ask participants to write down any questions they have during the DVD presentation so that you can address them at the end of the class. Mention some of the many free resources available on The Way of the Master website and explain that a deeper review of each of the topics covered in this course is found in the *Conquer Your Fear, Share Your Faith* book.

Continue by taking a few minutes to read the following "Three Minutes to Live" script aloud to your group to put participants in the right mindset to watch "The Firefighter" presentation from Kirk Cameron and Ray Comfort. Allow them to ponder any questions that arise.

THREE MINUTES TO LIVE

Let me give you a scenario that will help set our focus for today's class.

There's a knife in my back, and I've got three minutes to live. Tell me how to be saved.

I plead with you, "I'm dying, help me—what can I do to enter heaven? Help me!"

We know that most Christians would flounder; they don't know what to say. What are you going to say if you encounter someone who has a knife in his back and has three minutes to live?

Are you going to say, "God has a wonderful plan for your life"? What are you going to say? You want to be a true and faithful witness; you don't want to adulterate the Word of God.

You don't want to cause this person to have a false conversion and end up in hell because he hasn't repented, because he hasn't understood sin.

Could you share the gospel in three minutes with a dying person?

You think, There's no way I'm going to meet someone with a knife in his back. I'm fine.

Listen, every day 150,000 people die. Every 24 hours, 150,000 people around the world are swallowed by death.

Odds are that one day you might find someone in the supermarket who is having a heart attack, and there in your arms he looks you in the eyes saying, "Help me, help me, I'm dying!"

What are you going to say to him? Have you prepared yourself?

Believe it or not, the ability to share the gospel biblically and effectively does not come intuitively.

Almost everything you do in life is something you've learned. You learned to walk; you learned to use a knife and fork; you learned how to ride a bike and drive a car . . .

In Ephesians 4:11-12, Paul says that the evangelist is for "the equipping of the saints." We need to be equipped. We need to study to show ourselves approved, workers who need not be ashamed. And of all the things we shouldn't be ashamed of, it's the gospel of salvation. There's no message more important that can pass through our lips than the gospel of eternal salvation.

Have you prepared yourself?

Who do you know that isn't saved? Your mom, your dad, your spouse, your children, friends, neighbors, coworkers . . . ?

Who do you know that isn't saved?

The reality is that any one of us may have only three minutes to live—none of us is guaranteed even the next heartbeat.

© 2009 Kirk Cameron and Ray Comfort. Permission to photocopy granted.

We don't know when will be the last time we speak with someone.

All of us are living on "death row." It's not a pleasant thought, but it's the truth.

And the reality is that if people die in their sins, they will be spending eternity in hell.

We must have an urgency; we must equip ourselves.

We want to lay a foundation for you today that we believe will be life changing. But please understand that this is a foundation–you will need to build upon this foundation for the rest of your life.

Don't wait to start talking with others until you feel "ready"–all of us struggle with feeling ready. Instead, become "more ready" every day–more equipped today than you were yesterday, more equipped today than you were last year.

So with that encouragement, let's get started!

© 2009 Kirk Cameron and Ray Comfort. Permission to photocopy granted.

Tell participants that in the first DVD, Kirk Cameron and Ray Comfort will tell the story of a firefighter who was charged with neglect in the line of duty. The firefighter's neglect caused the needless and tragic deaths of a family of five. Remind participants to turn off cell phones and refrain from getting up during the video. Then show "The Firefighter" DVD to the class.

Break

Announce that there will be a 15-minute break. Invite participants to get a snack, and remind them of the location of the restrooms if needed. During the break, have each participant complete the session 1 quiz. Watch the clock and start promptly after 15 minutes to be respectful of your group's time.

SESSION 4 QUIZ

1. How did you react as you heard the firefighter's story? What did the firefighter do that was wrong?

   _____

   _____

   _____

   _____

2. Can you think of any justification for his lack of concern?

   _____

   _____

   _____

   _____

3. Was the fire chief justified in dishonorably discharging the firefighter from the fire department? What sentence did you give the firefighter?

   _____

   _____

   _____

   _____

4. Who are the people in your life whose salvation you are most concerned about?

   _____

   _____

   _____

   _____

5. Why are you concerned?

   _____

   _____

   _____

   _____

6. What are you doing about it?

_____

_____

_____

_____

7. With whom do you find it more difficult to share the gospel: family and friends, or complete strangers? Why?

_____

_____

_____

_____

8. How would you describe your current attitude about the fate of the lost: (a) unconcerned; (b) concerned; (c) alarmed; (d) horrified? Why?

_____

_____

_____

_____

9. Did you find it helpful to see someone on the program witnessing? Why or why not?

_____

_____

_____

_____

Conclude by writing a letter to God. Say something like, "God, these are my hopes and desires for this course. This is what I'm afraid of and this is what I'm hoping You'll do in me." Then write out what you want to see God do in your life through these lessons. Seal it in an envelope and place your name on it. No one is going to read it. Give it to the leader for safekeeping. It will be returned to you at the end of the course, and you will then see how God answered your prayers. Be sure to do this because it will be a very meaningful experience when you graduate.

Discussion Time

Now have the group participants take a few minutes to discuss their quiz answers with the small group. (**Note:** If you are meeting with a large group, break your large group into groups of three to five people and discuss your answers to the session one quiz.)

Q&A Time

Before you wrap up session 1, ask participants if they have any questions about the session, the quiz or "The Firefighter" DVD. Have a couple of trusted fishermen help you answer questions if necessary. If participants have any specific or detailed concerns, refer to the Q&A section of this Leader's Guide (page 81) for answers about the evangelism strategies outlined in this guide. (**Note:** It might be helpful to copy the questions and answers in the back of this guide and hand them out to the group at the end of the session.)

Optional: Homework Assignment
(Use for the four-week course option)

Thank everyone for participating in the first session, and encourage each person to read chapters 1-4 in the *Conquer Your Fear, Share Your Faith* book before session 2.

SESSION

2

HELL'S BEST KEPT SECRET

Optional: Welcome/Prayer
(Use for the four-week course option)

Welcome participants to session 2 of the *Conquer Your Fear, Share Your Faith* course. Open in prayer, asking God to bless your time together and to encourage the participants as you continue in this course.

Testimonials

Have two people (yourself, or other trusted evangelists or fishermen) share their evangelism testimonies for roughly 3 to 5 minutes each. Specifically ask them to talk about how they overcame their fears in order to share their faith with another person individually, or other people in a group setting.

"Hell's Best Kept Secret" DVD

In the second DVD, Ray Comfort teaches on the lost key to the sinner's heart. It's called "Hell's Best Kept Secret." You can introduce the DVD by saying something similar to the following: "Why do 80 to 90 percent of those making a decision for Christ fall away from the faith? What is the principle that Spurgeon, Wesley, Whitefield and other great preachers used to reach the lost? Why has the Church neglected it? Get ready to discover what Charles Spurgeon called 'our ablest auxiliary'—that is, our most powerful weapon!"

To remove any "shock" over the evangelism style the participants will see, explain the difference between open-air preaching and one-on-one conversations. Open-air preaching requires the speaker to shout or preach loudly so the crowd can hear the speaker, and sometimes requires a harsher tone than in the gentler, more intimate one-to-one encounters. Point out that even though participants will learn from these conversations, they will *not* be expected to open-air preach. Remind participants to turn off cell phones and refrain from getting up during the video. Then show the "Hell's Best Kept Secret" DVD to the class.

Break

Announce that there will be a 15-minute break. Invite participants to get a snack, and remind them of the location of the restrooms if needed. During the break, have each participant complete the session 2 quiz. Watch the clock and start promptly after 15 minutes to be respectful of your group's time.

SESSION 2 QUIZ

1. What is it that the Bible says is "perfect, converting the soul"? (See Psalm 19:7.)

   _____

   _____

   _____

   _____

   _____

2. According to Romans 3:19-20, Romans 7:7 and Galatians 3:24, what are four functions of the Law?

   1. _____

   2. _____

   3. _____

   4. _____

3. What is the biblical definition of sin? (See 1 John 3:4.)

   _____

   _____

   _____

   _____

4. What does the word "conscience" mean?

   _____

   _____

   _____

   _____

5. What did modern evangelism choose to use to attract sinners to the gospel?

   _____

   _____

   _____

   _____

6. What was the first passenger told about the parachute?

_____

_____

_____

_____

_____

7. What was the result of his experience?

_____

_____

_____

_____

8. What was the second passenger told?

_____

_____

_____

_____

9. What was the result of his experience?

_____

_____

_____

_____

10. What should we be telling the "passengers"?

_____

_____

_____

_____

11. Who is the Law designed for (see 1 Timothy 1:9-10)?

_____

_____

_____

_____

BONUS: How many of the Ten Commandments can you name by memory?

1. _____
2. _____
3. _____
4. _____
5. _____
6. _____
7. _____
8. _____
9. _____
10. _____

SESSION 2 QUIZ ANSWERS

1. The Law of the Lord is perfect converting the soul. Matthew Henry says, "Nothing is to be added to it nor taken from it. It is of use to convert the soul, to bring us back to ourselves, to our God, to our duty; for it shows us our sinfulness and misery in our departures from God and the indispensable necessity of our return to him."

2. Four of the functions of God's Law for humanity are: (1) it stops the sinner's mouth from justifying itself; (2) it makes the whole world realize that they are guilty; (3) it brings the knowledge of sin; and (4) it acts as a schoolmaster to bring us to Christ.

3. The biblical definition of sin is transgression of the Law. This is the definition of sin in general. The Greek word "sin" (*hamartia*) is literally "a missing of the mark" (God's perfect Law is the mark that we must aim for). Romans 3:20 tells us, "By the law is the knowledge of sin." The straight edge of a ruler shows the crookedness of a line.

4. The word "conscience" means "with knowledge." *Con* means "with" and *science* means "knowledge."

5. Modern evangelism has chosen to attract sinners by using "benefits." Life enhancement is now the drawing card to bring someone to Christ, with something like this: "You will never find true happiness until you come to the Lord. You have a 'God-shaped vacuum' that only He can fill. God will heal your marriage and take away that addiction problem. He'll get you out of financial trouble and be your best friend."

6. The first passenger was told that the parachute would improve his flight.

7. He put the parachute on for the wrong reason. He became disillusioned and somewhat embittered against the person who gave him the parachute, and quite rightly so. He was promised the parachute would improve the flight and all he got was embarrassment and humiliation.

8. He was told the parachute would save his life.

9. The second passenger didn't notice the extra weight upon his shoulders or the fact that he couldn't sit upright. He was able to withstand the mockery of the other passengers because he didn't put the parachute on for a better flight, but rather to escape the jump to come. Everything else just paled in comparison to the horrific thought of having to jump without the parachute.

10. We should be telling the other passengers they have an appointment with death they will not miss. Unless they repent and put on the Lord Jesus Christ, they will die in their sins. They need to know they are enemies of God through their wicked works and that God will judge them in righteousness.

11. The Law is designed for lawbreakers and rebels, the ungodly and sinful, the unholy and irreligious; for those who kill their fathers or mothers, for murderers, for adulterers and perverts, for slave traders and liars and perjurers—and for whatever else is contrary to the sound doctrine.

BONUS answer:
1. You shall have no other gods before Me.
2. You shall not make for yourself an idol.
3. You shall not take the name of God in vain.
4. Remember the Sabbath day to keep it holy.
5. Honor your father and your mother.
6. You shall not murder.
7. You shall not commit adultery.
8. You shall not steal.
9. You shall not bear false witness (lie).
10. You shall not covet.

Discussion Time

Have your group answer the following two questions. (**Note:** If you are meeting with a large group, break your large group into groups of three to five people.) You might want to copy this page before the meeting and hand out copies of the questions (but not the answers!) to each small group.

Question 1: How can I overcome my fear of witnessing?

Question 2: What do you do when a Christian friend is falling out of the will of God? He knows the Ten Commandments but doesn't see anything wrong with what he is doing and gets angry when I try to talk to him about it.

After the groups have discussed the questions for about 5 minutes, ask each group to share their answers to each question. After each group has shared (or each person if you're in a small group), share the answers below from Kirk and Ray.

Question 1: There are a number of ways to overcome fear. First, realize that it is spiritual. The Bible speaks of it as "the spirit of fear." You are going to have to fight it every time you step out of your comfort zone. So don't listen to the enemy. Instead, be prayerful, and let love for the unsaved swallow your fears. See yourself as a brave firefighter who beats back fear because he wants to rescue a child from the flames.

Question 2: If the friend is willfully getting into sin, this is a sign of a false conversion. Send him a loving letter, explaining that you are deeply concerned for him. (You might also want to read 1 John 1–3 and Matthew 7.)

Q&A Time

Before you wrap up session 2, ask participants if they have any questions about the session, the quiz or the "Hell's Best Kept Secret" DVD. Have a couple of trusted fishermen help you answer questions if necessary. If participants have any specific or detailed concerns, refer to the Q&A section of this Leader's Guide (page 81) for answers about the evangelism strategies outlined in this guide. (**Note:** It might be helpful to copy the questions and answers in the back of this guide and hand them out to the group at the end of the session.)

Optional: Homework Assignment
(Use for the four-week course option)

Thank everyone for participating in the second session, and encourage each person to read Chapters 5–8 in their *Conquer Your Fear, Share Your Faith* books before session 3.

SESSION

3

TRUE & FALSE CONVERSIONS

Optional: Welcome/Prayer

(Use for the four-week course option)

Welcome participants to session 3 of the *Conquer Your Fear, Share Your Faith* course. Open in prayer, asking God to bless your time together and to encourage the participants as you continue in this course.

"True & False Conversions" DVD

In this DVD, Ray Comfort will teach on a subject that is critical to winning souls yet is rarely mentioned in churches today. Ask participants to consider the state of the Church as they watch this DVD presentation—it has the same illegitimate pregnancy and abortion rate as the world, the same divorce rate, the same rebellious behavior from youth, and so forth. Ask them why it is that the Church is watching the same movies and listening to the same music as the world. Why are just as many men trapped in pornography inside the Church as outside? Remind them to consider these things as they watch this segment. Then show the "True & False Conversions" DVD to the class.

Break

Announce that there will be a 15-minute break. Invite participants to get a snack, and remind them of the location of the restrooms if needed. During the break, have each participant complete the session 3 quiz. Watch the clock and start promptly after 15 minutes to be respectful of your group's time.

SESSION 3 QUIZ

1. What damage can be done by a Christian who doesn't understand that there is such a thing as a false conversion?

   _____

   _____

   _____

   _____

2. What did Jesus say to His disciples when questioned about the Parable of the Sower?

   _____

   _____

   _____

   _____

3. In the Parable of the Sower, what are the six characteristics of a false convert?

   _____

   _____

   _____

   _____

4. What light does James 2:19 shed on the sixth characteristic of a false convert?

   _____

   _____

   _____

   _____

5. What are the five fruits of a true convert?

   1. _____

   2. _____

   3. _____

   4. _____

   5. _____

6. What are the three things that happen here on earth to expose false converts?

   1. _____
   2. _____
   3. _____

7. When will the false convert ultimately be exposed?

   _____
   _____
   _____
   _____

8. Name some parables that Jesus told that speak of true and false conversions.

   _____
   _____
   _____
   _____

9. How can we, as evangelistic Christians, make sure we are not responsible for bringing false converts into the Church?

   _____
   _____
   _____
   _____

BONUS: What "false" person do the following verses warn us about?

   Matthew 7:15
   Mark 13:22
   2 Corinthians 11:13
   Galatians 2:4
   2 Peter 2:1

SESSION 3 QUIZ ANSWERS

1. The damage done by a Christian who doesn't understand there is such a thing as a false conversion can be devastating. If we lack understanding that those who fail to repent are strangers to conversion, we're liable to think that simply praying a sinner's prayer or responding to an altar call gets someone saved.

2. Jesus told His disciples when they questioned Him about the Parable of the Sower, "Do you not understand this parable? How then will you understand all the parables?" (Mark 4:13). In other words, the Parable of the Sower is the key to unlocking the mysteries of all the other parables.

3. Six characteristics of a false convert in the Parable of the Sower:

   1. Immediate results (Mark 4:5)
   2. Lack of moisture (Luke 8:6)
   3. No root (Matthew 13:6)
   4. Receives the word with gladness (Mark 4:16)
   5. Receives the word with joy (Matthew 13:20)
   6. They do "believe" for a season (Luke 8:13)

4. James 2:19 says, "You believe that there is one God. You do well. Even the demons believe—and tremble!" This verse reveals that mere belief—when not accompanied by repentance (Luke 13:3) and placing one's faith in Christ (Acts 20:21)—is not sufficient for salvation.

5. Five fruits of a true convert:

   1. Fruit of repentance (Matthew 3:8)
   2. Fruit of thanksgiving (Hebrews 13:15)
   3. Fruit of good works (Colossians 1:10)
   4. Fruit of the Spirit (Galatians 5:22-23)
   5. Fruit of righteousness (Philippians 1:11)

6. Tribulation, temptation, and persecution.

7. The false convert will be exposed as a hypocrite on Judgment Day, when the wheat and the tares will be separated.

8. The Wheat and Tares (true and false), the Good Fish and Bad Fish (true and false), the Foolish Virgins and the Wise Virgins (true and false), and the Sheep and Goats (true and false).

9. We can make sure we are not responsible for bringing false converts into the Church by making it paramount to preach biblically. That means using the Law to bring a knowledge of sin. It means mentioning Judgment Day, not casually, but impressing upon the mind of our hearer that he must face a holy God and answer for every sin he has committed against Him. It also means preaching the cross and the necessity of repentance. We should avoid modern methods where emotions are stirred in an effort to get decisions. We may rejoice over decisions, but heaven reserves its rejoicing for repentance.

BONUS answer:

Matthew 7:15: False prophets
Mark 13:22: False christs
2 Corinthians 11:13: False apostles
Galatians 2:4: False brethren
2 Peter 2:1: False teachers

Discussion Time

Have your group answer the following two questions. (**Note:** If you are meeting with a large group, break your large group into groups of three to five people.) You might want to copy this page before the meeting and hand out copies of the questions (but not the answers!) to each small group.

Question 1: After leading people to Christ, how do you follow up with them? What tools do you give for them to develop their own personal relationship with Christ?

Question 2: What is the difference between "follow up" and "discipleship"?

After the groups have discussed the questions for about 5 minutes, ask each group to share their answers to each question. After each group has shared (or each person if you're in a small group), share the answers below from Kirk and Ray.

Question 1: If someone truly comes to Christ, it is a work of God. And if he or she is "born of God," God will take care of that person, with or without our follow up. Nevertheless, you might want to give any new converts the booklet "Save Yourself Some Pain," which contains 10 principles for Christian growth. There, they will find encouragement to read the Bible daily and obey it, share their faith, get into fellowship, and so forth. To help the person find a good church, you may want to get some contact information so you can send him or her details about the nearest church. Then ask the pastor of that fellowship to contact the person and extend a personal invitation to his church.

Question 2: Follow up is running after a professed believer, while discipleship is living the Christian life. Follow up occurs when we get decisions, either through crusades or local church services, and take laborers from the harvest field (who are few as it is) and give them the disheartening task of running after these "decisions" to make sure they're continuing with God. Discipling is simply encouraging a person to lead a Christian life. While feeding, nurturing and discipling a new convert is important—it's biblical and necessary—it is not necessary to follow up with him or her.

Q&A Time

Before you wrap up session 3, ask participants if they have any questions about the session, the quiz or the "True & False Conversions" DVD. Have a couple of trusted fishermen help you answer questions if necessary. If participants have any specific or detailed concerns, refer to the Q&A section of this Leader's Guide (page 81) for answers about the evangelism strategies outlined in this guide. (**Note:** It might be helpful to copy the questions and answers in the back of this guide and hand them out to the group at the end of the session.)

Optional: Homework Assignment

(Use for the four-week course option)

Thank everyone for participating in the third session of this course and encourage each person to read chapters 9-12 in addition to chapter 16 (which is on the topic of true conversion) in their *Conquer Your Fear, Share Your Faith* books before the fourth and final session.

SESSION

4

WHAT DID JESUS DO?

Optional: Welcome/Prayer

(Use for the 4-week course option)

Welcome participants to session 4, the final session of the *Conquer Your Fear, Share Your Faith* course! Open in prayer, asking God to bless your time together and your upcoming fishing trips both as a group and individually.

"What Did Jesus Do?" DVD

In the fourth DVD, you'll see both Kirk and Ray in Venice Beach, California, putting the *Conquer Your Fear, Share Your Faith* principles into practice face-to-face with non-Christians. Explain that the video doesn't show entire conversations but is intended to demonstrate how to witness using the principles outlined in this course. Have participants watch for people who seem familiar with part of the gospel but have no real understanding of what Jesus did for them. Don't make the mistake of thinking that everyone in the United States has heard the gospel—even those who have some church experience may not understand the cross if the do not have the Law to help them see their sin and their need for a Savior. Now show the "What Did Jesus Do?" DVD to the class.

Break

Announce that there will be a 15-minute break. Invite participants to get a snack, and remind them of the location of the restrooms if needed. During the break, have each participant complete the session 4 quiz. Watch the clock and start promptly after 15 minutes to be respectful of your group's time.

SESSION 4 QUIZ

Read this article, and then answer the questions that follow it.

Personal Witnessing–What Did Jesus Do?

To share our faith effectively, we must show people that we care by being friendly. Practice on people at the park, gas station, or grocery store, with a simple, "Hi, how are you?" or, "Good morning! Nice day, isn't it?" If the person responds warmly, we may then ask, "Do you live around here?" and develop a conversation.

In talking with the woman at the well, Jesus began in the natural realm (everyday things). You may want to do the same by talking about sports or the weather, then perhaps using something in the news to transition to spiritual things. Another simple way to swing to the spiritual is to offer a gospel tract and ask, "Did you get one of these?" When the person takes it, say, "It's a gospel tract. Do you have a Christian background?"

Then by following the WDJD outline, you can confidently lead any witnessing encounter. You'll know exactly where you are in a conversation and exactly where it is going. You can say goodbye to your fears! Let's follow the way of the Master given in Luke 18:18-21. Jesus first addressed the man's understanding of good.

W: Would you consider yourself to be a good person?

People are not offended by this question, because you are asking about their favorite subject—themselves. Expect them to respond, "Yes, I'm a pretty good person." This reveals their pride and self-righteousness. At this point you are ready to use the Law (the Ten Commandments) to humble them . . . the way Jesus did.

D: Do you think you have kept the Ten Commandments?

With the rich, young ruler, Jesus used the Law to bring "the knowledge of sin" (Romans 3:20). We can do the same by asking this question. Most people think they have, so follow with, "Let's take a look at a few and see. Have you ever told a lie?" This may seem confrontational, but if asked in a spirit of love, there won't be any offense. Remember that the "work of the Law [is] written in their hearts" and their conscience will bear "witness" (Romans 2:15). Have confidence that the conscience will do its work and affirm the truth of each Commandment.

Some will admit to lying; others will say they have told only "white lies." Ask, "What does that make you?" They will hesitate to say, but get them to admit, "A liar." Continue going through the Commandments. Ask, "Have you ever stolen something, even if it's small?" Ask, "What does that make you?" and press them to say, "A thief." Say, "Jesus said, 'Whoever looks at a woman to lust for her has already committed adultery with her in his heart.' Have you ever looked at someone with lust?"

Then ask, "Have you ever taken the Lord's name in vain?" Gently explain, "So instead of using a four-letter filth word to express disgust, you've taken the name of the One who gave you life and everything that is precious to you, and you have dragged it through the mud. That's called 'blasphemy,' and God promises that He will not hold anyone blameless who takes His name in vain."

At this point, the individual will either grow quiet (his "mouth may be stopped" by the Law, Romans 3:19) or will be getting agitated. Ask his name and say, "John, by your own admission, you're a lying thief, a blasphemer, and an adulterer at heart, and we've only looked at four of the Ten Commandments."

J–Judgment: If God judges you by the Ten Commandments on the Day of Judgment, will you be innocent or guilty?

If he says he will be innocent, say, "You just told me that you broke God's Law. Think about it. Will you be innocent or guilty?" It's very important that you get an admission of guilt.

D–Destiny: Will you go to heaven or hell?

People won't be offended because you are simply asking a question, rather than telling them where they're going. From there the conversation may go one of three ways:

1. *He may confidently say, "I don't believe in hell."* Gently respond, "That doesn't matter. You still have to face God on Judgment Day whether you believe in it or not. If I step onto the freeway when a massive truck is heading for me and I say, 'I don't believe in trucks,' my lack of belief isn't going to change reality."

2. *He may admit he's guilty, but say he'll go to heaven.* He may think God is "good" and will therefore overlook sin in his case. Point out that if a judge has a guilty murderer standing before him, if he's a good judge, he can't just let him go. He must ensure that the guilty man is punished. If God is good, He must punish murderers, rapists, thieves, liars, adulterers, and those who live in rebellion to the inner light God has given every man. Tenderly tell him he has already admitted that he's

lied, stolen, blasphemed, and committed adultery in his heart, and that God gave him a conscience so he'd know right from wrong.

3. *He may admit that he is guilty and therefore going to hell.* Ask if that concerns him. Speak about how much he values his eyes and how much more therefore he should value the salvation of his soul.

To give him the good news, follow the outline CCRAFT: Concern, Cross, Repentance And Faith, Truth. If the person has been humbled and admits he's concerned, then you have the privilege of sharing the cross with him, encouraging him to repent and place his faith in the Savior. If he's willing to confess and forsake his sins, have him pray and ask God to forgive him. Then pray for him. Point him to the truth of the Bible, instructing him to read it daily and obey what he reads, and get into a Bible-believing church.

1. How should you begin talking with an unbeliever?

   _____

   _____

   _____

2. Give two possible ways you could swing the conversation to the spiritual.

   _____

   _____

   _____

3. Tell how you would bring conviction using the Law.

   _____

   _____

   _____

   _____

4. How should you give the good news to a sinner?

   _____

   _____

   _____

   _____

For the answers to this quiz, simply review the article.

Demonstrate Tracts/Role-Play

Next, have the group break into pairs do some brief evangelistic role-playing. In this exercise, the participants will use gospel tracts as an icebreaker to start a conversation with another person. You can do this exercise with the *Way of the Master* tracts or even tracts of your own, but you'll want to give your groups suggestions for how to use them.

Depending on the makeup of your group, you might want to model a sample role-play with a coleader. If you do, begin by asking, "Did you get one of these?" as you hand a tract to the other person. After the person takes the tract, explain that it is a gospel tract and then ask, "Did you grow up in religious household?" or, "Have you ever gone to church before?"

As the other person looks at the tract, open up the discussion by asking, "Would you consider yourself to be a good person?" or "What do you think happens when someone dies? Do you think you'll go to heaven?" You can follow this up with another question: "Would you consider yourself to be a good person?"

If you are demonstrating the million-dollar bill tracts, you might say: "This has a million-dollar question on the back that's even more valuable! So, do you think you'll go to heaven?" However, regardless of what tract you use, you can say, "This has an important message on it. Please take some time to read it." Be sure to give enough time so that everyone has a chance to practice opening up a conversation.

Closing Remarks

Take a few minutes at the close of the course to talk about the fishing trip you will schedule after the final session. This is an optional event, but one we greatly encourage you to schedule so that your group can see these principles in action (and perhaps even try them!).

Encourage participants to join you on the fishing trip, but do not require them to speak with anyone. The purpose of the trip is for them to simply watch and listen to you and other experienced fishermen share the gospel. If they are ready to take a step out of their comfort zone, they can choose to hand out tracts or even dive in and begin talking with others.

Let participants know that you will be notifying them of any future fishing trips, training courses and ongoing training opportunities. Explain that you will send them a list of today's attendees, and encourage them to get together with someone else from class and begin to make evangelism a way of life. There is nothing more exciting!

Optional: Homework Assignment
(Use for the four-week course option)

Although this is the final session, encourage participants to read chapters 13-15 and chapter 17 (on the fruit of biblical evangelism) in *Conquer Your Fear, Share Your Faith* on their own.

Closing Prayer

Close the meeting in prayer, asking God to bless each person in attendance and their future evangelistic endeavors.

Q & A

The following are questions that we have received over the years about our teaching on evangelism. Read through this material to give you an idea of how to answer certain questions that your participants might raise during the Q&A in the course.

PREPARATION

Save some, O Christians! By all means, save some. From yonder flames and outer darkness,
and the weeping, wailing, and gnashing of teeth, seek to save some! Let this, as in the case of the apostle,
be your great, ruling object in life, that by all means you might save some.

CHARLES SPURGEON

(1)

I struggle with having confidence to go in front of someone and share the gospel. I just don't know if I know enough to go out and do that. How do you overcome this fear?

You can't use lack of knowledge as an excuse for not sharing your faith, because what is "enough"? All you need to know is the basics of the gospel. Never worry about some intellectual stumping you with a question you can't answer. You can always say, "I'm sorry. I don't know the answer to that." The truth is that you will never know how to do it until you do it. So you must ignore your fears; they will leave the moment you begin. (I still have fear after all these years.) Start in the natural (maybe the death of a famous actor, or some news item or trivia) and then swing to the fact that we will all die and be judged by the Commandments. Go through the Law and preach the cross, repentance and faith. Then say, "Thank you for listening." Look on it as a learning experience at first. You are needed. People are going to hell, and the laborers are few to tell them how to keep from going to hell.

(2)

I know God wants me to share my faith, but I feel that if I don't, God doesn't love me and I cannot maintain a relationship with Him. If we are saved by faith and not by works, why can't I have that relationship with God without witnessing?

This is an honest question. Here is the problem: We know we are saved because the fruit of God's Spirit begins manifesting through us. God is love; therefore, we should be filled with love if we have been truly saved (see Romans 5:5). Think of this scenario: You are in Africa. A child is lying on the ground in front of you, starving to death. You have food in your hand. You know God wants you to share the food with the dying child. So the question is, *Why can't I have a good relationship with God without sharing the food?* You have to answer that for yourself.

3

I want so much to share my faith and testimony, to speak in churches and share God's Word in the evangelist field. However, I haven't written a book (yet) and my name isn't known. How can I do this?

Ask God to open doors for you, and in the meanwhile, busy yourself doing menial things. Be a servant. My first international invitation to speak came when I was painting a restroom at a church. The second came when I was pushing a stranger's car because it would not start. That spoke volumes to me about God honoring us when we are servants. So go wash feet.

4

Why do Christians have so much fear and hardship proclaiming the truth when the cults and other religions have no troubling proclaiming lies?

It's important to remember that we fight a spiritual battle. Whenever we approach some-one with the gospel, we battle the spirit of fear. However, those in cults and other religions are not wrestling against demonic forces. There is no battle for them. Instead of fighting against the enemy, they are fighting for him. But they also have another incentive. Their public agenda is to spread what they believe is the truth, but their *motive* is one of self-advancement. They don't believe that they will enter the kingdom unless they add works to their faith, so that becomes a strong incentive and energizer. The Christian, however, has a nobler motive. We reach out to the lost because we love God and because we are deeply concerned (horrified) at the fate of the unsaved.

5

As a married woman, am I supposed to zealously witness the way that Paul and the other apostles did? I am referring to Scriptures like 1 Timothy 2:9-15 and 1 Peter 3:1-6. I do believe that the husband is the head of the wife.

Jesus calls everyone—both men and women—to share their faith. Just don't get into a posi-tion where you are exercising authority over men. Dress modestly, obey your husband and make sure that you share your faith whenever and wherever you can. If your husband is not a Christian, then be a prayer warrior and give out tracts and witness as much as you can without offending him and harming your relationship.

6

I'm alone in my efforts in biblical evangelism in my city. Other Christians say they appreciate what I'm doing by going out on the streets but think it's because I have a "gift" for evangelism. They say it's not their gift or calling, so they'll just stay in their comfort zone and pray for me. They hide behind Ephesians 4:11: "He Himself gave some to be apostles, some prophets, some evangelists, and some pastors and teachers." How do I convince them that everyone is called to evangelism?

Point out to them that some are called to be evangelists "for the equipping of the *saints* for the work of ministry" (Ephesians 4:12, emphasis added). All Christians (saints) are commanded to evangelize. We have a moral obligation to do so. How can any person who professes to love God have no concern that sinners are going to hell? To encourage and equip other believers to step out of their comfort zone to reach the lost, you may want to invite some to study this course or the *Conquer Your Fear, Share Your Faith* book in your home or church. Pray that God would raise up laborers, and see what you can do to help.

7

Is it wise to send new converts out into the battlefield before they are grounded in the Word and apologetics?

It is the best thing you can do for them. The woman at the well didn't go to a seminary before she testified of the Savior, and she brought a whole village to Him. After finding Christ, Andrew immediately told Simon Peter. The first thing Philip did was to find Nathanael and immediately tell him about the Savior (see John 1:35-51). If new converts came to Christ under the sound of the Law, they know enough to go and do likewise with the lost. They will make mistakes. They may get bruised. But that is how we learned to walk as toddlers, and the same is true spiritually.

8

I was saved three years ago after listening to the "Hell's Best Kept Secret" message. Since then I have been bent on soul winning, but I've not been received well by my church or really anyone in the Christian family (although I am by the lost). Still, I pray God gives me strength to push myself to witness in the steps of Christ. Do you have any advice?

You are not alone. There are many who find themselves almost isolated, simply because they are deeply burdened to reach the lost, and they want to do it biblically. That's one of the reasons we have the Ambassadors' Alliance (see www.ambassadorsalliance.com), to encourage those who find themselves in such circumstances.

9

How would you deal with a church staff and members who are not compassionate about soul-winning or who do not believe in this type of winning the lost? Should I leave my church?

That, ultimately, has to be your decision. But I would add that you should hang in there as long as you can. Who knows what changes God could bring in your church through your prayers and perseverance. If you find yourself getting bitter or too frustrated, find another church that has a love for the unsaved. Ask God to give you wisdom so that you make the right decision, keeping in mind that you want a church to have a positive influence on your family.

10

I have been a pastor for six years. God has given me the honor of leading a number of people to the Lord in my office when they come onto my turf for counsel. However, your show has inspired me to take the gospel to the streets. How can I overcome my fear of witnessing on the sinner's turf?

There are a number of ways to overcome fear. First, realize that it is spiritual. The Bible speaks of it as "the spirit of fear." You are going to have to fight it every time you step out of your comfort zone. So don't listen to the enemy. Instead, be prayerful, and let love for the unsaved swallow your fears. See yourself as a brave firefighter who beats back fear because he wants to rescue a child from the flames.

11

I sometimes seem to "offend" people when I share my faith. They say that I am attacking them. How can I effectively share the good news without offending others? I realize that Jesus offended a lot of people, and I'm not worried about the effect of truth, but I would just like to be more effective for my Lord.

You are right about the fact that there is a natural offense with the gospel, but perhaps it could also be your tone. Are you an "intense" person? We're called to speak with gentleness and respect, so be sure your attitude is one of humble compassion. Do you take a moment to build a bridge with an unsaved person before you swing to spiritual things? Do you use a little humor before you transition to the things of God? (Some of our tracts can do that for you, if you are not personally inclined that way.) Ask a close Christian friend to listen as you witness to someone and see what he thinks.

12

I've been out on the street witnessing for about three years now, and I can't say confidently that I have ever seen anyone "saved." I've seen so many people cry and appear convicted, but none of them have ever called me or written about how their new faith is going. So the question is: What do you do when you feel like you're not doing anything at all?

This is such a good question, because you are going to have people come up to you and say things like, "I led 169 people to the Lord last week, praise the Lord. All glory to Him for what He's doing!" And there you are, faithfully laboring away, and you haven't seen anyone come to the Lord.

More than likely, the main reason that you don't see "decisions" for Christ is that you fear God. And because of that healthy fear of the Lord, you don't want to lead a single soul into a false profession of faith. We know how easy it is to get decisions and impress people with numbers, but we also know better. It would be easy to say to those who have heard the gospel, "Do you know for sure that your name is written in heaven? Would you like to have that knowledge? I could lead you in a sinner's prayer right now, so you can know that when you die you will go to heaven. Would you like to pray?" God forbid that you and I would contribute to the numbers of tares that are sitting among the wheat in the contemporary Church.

I preached the gospel for 12 years almost daily and hardly saw a soul come to Christ. However, after I left New Zealand and came to the United States, I started to hear of ones surrendering to Christ who had listened to the gospel so long ago.

So here is the way to keep yourself encouraged. See yourself as sowing in tears, then read these verses over and over, until you are familiar with them and understand them:

And he who reaps receives wages, and gathers fruit for eternal life, that both he who sows and he who reaps may rejoice together. For in this the saying is true: "One sows and another reaps." I sent you to reap that for which you have not labored; others have labored, and you have entered into their labors (John 4:36-38).

Therefore, my beloved brethren, be steadfast, immovable, always abounding in the work of the Lord, knowing that your labor is not in vain in the Lord (1 Corinthians 15:58).

Never be discouraged. Keep asking God that you may see fruit for your labors, but don't let seeing fruit now be your source of encouragement and motivation. Let it simply be the fact that God is faithful to watch over His Word. There's nothing wrong with the seed of the gospel, but it's up to God to cause it to bring life, in His perfect timing. You will see fruit *in eternity*. That's were it counts.

13

What should I do to prepare myself for going out witnessing?

One way to always be prepared is to constantly think about the fate of the unsaved. Think of yourself as a person living in the heart of a terrible drought. You have been given a supply of food and water to share. So how do you prepare yourself? You make sure you have food at hand for when you see someone who is starving to death. Our "food" is the gospel. That's what we want to get into the heart of dying humanity. You can use gospel tracts to get their mouths open. So, here's a summary: (1) be prayerful, (2) carry tracts, and (3) go over the gospel in your mind until you know how to present it biblically in 3 minutes, or in 30 minutes.

Those who use the excuse that they don't know what to say are perhaps those referred to in Scripture as being "ashamed" of the gospel. They are usually those who have never studied to show themselves approved as "a worker who does not need to be ashamed" (2 Timothy 2:15). Don't let that be true of you.

14

Our motive for sharing and reaching out to the lost must be the love of Jesus. If it is anything else, our motive will be exposed and we'll be ineffective. How can we be sure that our hearts are in the right place before hitting the streets?

Ask God to search out your motives. However, I would add one thing. Even if your heart isn't in the right place (I'm not talking about sin, but that you are going because of a sense of guilt), you should still go. If you were rescued from a burning building by a fireman who left the firehouse only because he felt guilty not coming to the fire, as far as you are concerned, his motive for rescuing you is not an issue. He did it. That's all that matters. So don't get hung up on why you reach out to the lost, just do it, while there is still time. The quality is in the seed, not the sower.

15

Can you describe your prayer life and what role that plays in your evangelism— that is, do you do any kind of prayer walking or such before evangelism?

For the last 25 years, I have gotten up most nights of the week (around midnight) to seek God in prayer. It hasn't been easy. The key is to go to bed early. When I get up to pray, I wrap a blanket around me and pray for about 30 minutes. Then I write for a couple of hours, read the Word and go back to sleep. I always have a pen and paper beside me when I pray. When our team leaves to do open-air preaching, we pray for God's help and His care for us driving the freeways. Just before we get up to preach, we pray. After the preaching, we pray for those who heard the Word that day.

16

How do you specifically pray for the lost?

I pray almost daily that God will raise up laborers. That's what Jesus told us to do: "The harvest truly is great, but the laborers are few; therefore pray the Lord of the harvest to send out laborers into His harvest" (Luke 10:2). That's the key to reaching the lost—more true and faithful laborers.

17

How do you keep yourself primed to reach the lost?

The Scriptures say, "But sanctify the Lord God in your hearts, and always be ready to give a defense to everyone who asks you a reason for the hope that is in you, with meekness and fear" (1 Peter 3:15). I thought that I was "always ready" to give an answer, but the other day I found that I wasn't.

I was riding my bike to work when I saw a gentleman walking on the sidewalk. As I rode past him, I offered him a Ten Commandments coin and said, "Did you get one of these?" He grabbed it from my hand and said, "Hey! Thank you very much!" He didn't know what it was, but he was so enthusiastic, I immediately wished I had stopped and engaged him in a conversation about the things of God. All the way to work I was kicking myself for not stopping, and I spent some time thinking about the incident. I came to the conclusion that I was not "always ready." I had a subconscious mentality of "hit and run." I needed to have a predetermined mindset to engage in a conversation, before I encountered anyone.

A few days later, I was riding to work when I saw a teenager on a skateboard heading for me. Suddenly, he slipped and sent the skateboard flying onto a busy road. He quickly ran out and retrieved it and jumped back onto the sidewalk. I said a friendly, "That was close!" and followed with, "Here's a million dollars for you." He smiled, and then I said, "It's a gospel tract. What do you think happens after someone dies? Do you think there's a heaven?" There was no offense on his part. He said, "I'm not sure." "Do you think there's a hell?" "Definitely." That reply was interesting. So we went through the Commandments, opening up their spiritual nature.

It turned out that he had lied, stolen, lusted and blasphemed God's name. He became rather sober, and it concerned him that because of his sins he was heading for hell. I then shared the good news that Jesus paid his fine and rose from the dead, and upon his repentance and faith in Jesus, God would grant him everlasting life. We shook hands. He went on his way, and I went on mine.

So if you are a chicken like me, and you fight inner fears, do yourself a big favor; deal with your fears in the prayer closet and predetermine to be ready. Always.

GETTING STARTED

If you never have sleepless hours, if you never have weeping eyes, if your hearts never swell as if they would burst, you need not anticipate that you will be called zealous. You do not know the beginning of true zeal, for the foundation of Christian zeal lies in the heart. The heart must be heavy with grief and yet must beat high with holy ardor. The heart must be vehement in desire, panting continually for God's glory, or else we shall never attain to anything like the zeal which God would have us know.

CHARLES SPURGEON

1

When you started to witness, did you take baby steps (like first getting comfortable handing out tracts) or did you take a giant "big boy" step and just start open-air preaching? What was the process you went through? Did you have someone there to mentor you?

Yes, I did take baby steps, and I did fall over and get bruised. However, right from the moment of my conversion, I was giving out tracts. If that's considered baby steps, then I'm still taking them. Rather than using the baby analogy, I would rather liken evangelism to swimming. My flesh still hates diving into a swimming pool. The moment I do so it is very uncomfortable, but my flesh adjusts to the water in seconds. It's the same with witnessing and open-air preaching—you have to will yourself to do it. Just do it. Dive in. It will make you grow like nothing else. No, I didn't have any mentor. My conscience was my coach. It drove me to do it.

The first time I open-air preached in the U.S. was off of a trash bin at Waikiki in Hawaii. Shortly after that I wandered among the sunbathers and said, "Hello, folks. My name is Ray. It must be a dream to lie on this famous beach and enjoy the warmth of the Hawaiian sun . . . and it would probably be a nightmare for a preacher to suddenly stand up and preach to you. But I have something extremely important to tell you, and I will be as quick as I can." I preached for about 20 minutes before a police officer approached me and said, "I have had eight complaints. You had better wind down." He was a Christian, so he patiently waited as long as he could, to give me more time to share the gospel.

2

Is it best to go out as Jesus sent the apostles, by twos?

You can, but it's not a rule. It seems that Paul preached by himself (such as on Mars Hill, see Acts 17:16-34). There is no mention of Stephen having a team or a partner. I've preached by myself for many years. If you're open-air preaching, sometimes it's easier to go by yourself; if you have a hard time at least you don't embarrass yourself in front of your friends. But if you're just getting your feet wet in witnessing, it's often helpful to go with a friend so that you can encourage one another.

3

My friend and I go to the local mall to witness for a few hours every week. Is it better to give out tracts to a lot of people or talk to only a few people in more depth?

Both are good. However, if I were to choose only one approach, I would lean toward one-to-one. Jesus went out of His way to talk one-to-one with the woman at the well (see John 4). He could have spent His valuable time preaching to multitudes, but He used it to speak to her personally, and alone. The problem is that we have a lack of laborers. I know of some people who find one-to-one difficult, but they can pass out tracts like a machine. These are the type of laborers you and your friend should take with you so your nets can be cast further.

4

What do you do if you live in a small town where there are only a few people at a time who walk down the street?

That's a difficult place to open-air preach. It may be best to hand out tracts and concentrate on witnessing one-to-one, or one-to-two. Make sure that you are rich in good works. Perhaps in winter you could stand somewhere giving out tracts with free hot chocolate, or with cool drinks in summer. Be sure to take advantage of any gatherings such as parades, citywide picnics and football games as well as county fairs and events in nearby cities. Even if these events are not conducive to open-air preaching, they're wonderful opportunities to give out plenty of tracts and witness one-to-one.

5

Do you go to certain planned events (such as air shows or parades), or do you stay away because you don't want to compete with them?

Any gatherings like parades and air shows are perfect for giving out tracts, especially our Giant Money tract. These tracts are so large that each person who gets one becomes a walking advertisement for them, and you will soon have people approach you and say, "So you're the one giving out those big $100 bills. May I have one?"

6

At public events, how do you witness to people individually? I've been to fairs, concerts and downtown celebrations to witness, and everybody there is with friends. I have witnessed to groups, but I think it's more effective one-to-one. What do you say when you approach a couple or a group of adults?

As you approach a group of two or more people and begin talking, often one person will be more friendly and responsive to you. To talk one-to-one, I simply address that person directly. It takes boldness to do this, but it seems to work, without offense. I say, "Let him speak. I want to know what he has to say." Often the rest of the group will get the hint and leave me to it. Speaking with a cooperative, interested person will allow you to share the gospel more effectively, while his companions can listen in.

7

How can I set up a debate against an atheist at our local college campus?

Check out the college's website and see if you can find any atheist or evolution group, and then challenge them to a debate. Make it worth their while by offering them $100 for their time. All they have to do is give their evidence as to why God doesn't exist, and you will give evidence as to why He does. Let the audience decide. Ask a Christian group on campus to promote it. You may even get the atheists to promote it as well. They will want it to be a success.

8

We go into a youth detention center to minister once a month, and the staff restricts our message so we can't mention hell, homosexuality or sin in general. Even though I have pushed the limits a few times, I'm careful to try to stay within their guidelines. How would you handle this situation?

Perhaps you could fill your message with analogies—about a criminal having his "fine" paid by a loving judge, and so forth. Maybe you could give them applicable verses by saying, "Here is this month's memory verse," and offer a free Bible to those who recite the verse(s) correctly the next time.

THE WAY OF THE MASTER METHOD

*Lower the Law and you dim the light by which man perceives his guilt; this is a very serious
loss to the sinner rather than a gain; for it lessens the likelihood of his conviction and conversion.
I say you have deprived the gospel of its ablest auxiliary [its most powerful weapon] when you
have set aside the Law. You have taken away from it the schoolmaster that is to bring men to Christ.*

CHARLES SPURGEON

1

Your message seems to be this: "Believe in Jesus and go to heaven, because you don't
want to go to hell." I think that this philosophy, while true literally, misses the true concept
that is found in Scripture. The reason to be a Christian and to serve God is not because "your
skin will be singed," as Reidhead wrote, but because the Lord is worthy of all glory.
We deserve hell, yet He has been merciful to us. How do you address this issue?

The unregenerate human heart is so desperately wicked, the motive for fleeing from wrath
should be honorable, but it's not. How could it be? The wicked criminal comes to be "saved"
because he is wicked. How can a vile sinner suddenly become virtuous in motive? It would
be admirable to have heard about the terrors of hell and not be fearful, and instead have
come to Christ because God is worthy of glory; but from where would a blind and lost sinner have found such theology? The truth is that there is nothing good in his own unregenerate and evil heart. That is the reason we preach the Law—to show the sinner the magnitude
of his crimes. Recognizing that he rightly deserves hell—but is offered mercy instead—is
what makes him respond in gratitude for all that Christ has done for him. Sinai produces
fear of God, because of His wrath. Calvary produces love for God, because of His mercy.

2

What scriptural proof can you offer that the way you witness to people is the way Jesus
witnessed? After all, you ask, "What *did* Jesus do?" and not "What *would* Jesus do?"

One example is in Mark 10, where the rich young ruler approached Jesus and asked what he
should do to get everlasting life. Jesus first reproved the man's understanding of the word

"good," then He showed him God's standards by going through five of the Ten Commandments. We have written an entire book called *What Did Jesus Do?* in answer to that question.

3

Even though I believe your witnessing style is effective and truly the way that Christ approached sharing the gospel, I sometimes think you believe born-again Christians aren't going to heaven unless they come to Christ through the Ten Commandments. Is that true?

All who have been born-again are going to heaven. For someone to come to Christ and be born again, he must repent. To repent, there must be knowledge of sin, and Paul said, "I would not have known sin except through the law" (Romans 7:7). All sin traces itself back to the Law, for "sin is the transgression of the law" (1 John 3:4, *KJV*). So I think the question is unfairly stated. It should rather be whether the principle we teach is biblical. If it isn't, drop it. If it is, embrace it with both hands.

4

What do you mean by "modern evangelism"? The statement that modern evangelism isn't working is vague. Are you including the popular "Steps to Peace with God" and Dr. James Kennedy's "Evangelism Explosion" approaches to reaching lost people?

The phrase "modern evangelism" is a generalization for the traditional evangelistic methods that are used by the contemporary Church but are unbiblical. The vagueness has been deliberate, because I don't want to criticize any ministry. Our motive is solely to reach the lost. I have the utmost admiration for the ministries you mentioned. However, when essential biblical principles have been omitted from any accepted and respected gospel presentation, we need to see what the Scriptures say on the subject and then align with the Word of God.

We may have the greatest admiration for a brilliant doctor, but if we know that he has made a mistake in a prescription by leaving out an essential ingredient, we have to set aside our admiration for the doctor and think of the welfare of the patient. It is clearly evident that the "patient" is deathly sick (by the patient, I don't mean the true Church, but rather the false converts that sit within the church—the "tares among the wheat," of which our churches are full). In January 2006, Dr. Kennedy aired "Hell's Best Kept Secret." He aired it twice in a year, the second time on "The Best of Truths That Transform." He would not have done so if the teaching was unbiblical or if he felt threatened or offended by it.

5

Isn't your approach a modern method as well?

May I respectfully say, "Test it against Scripture." Be a Berean with this (see Acts 17:11). It is based on foundational 2,000-year-old biblical principles. The use of the Law to bring the knowledge of sin is rooted in Holy Scripture. It may seem new to those who don't understand its true function, but it is definitely not "modern." To get you started, read Psalm 19:7; Romans 2:15; 3:19-20; 7:7; Galatians 3:24; 1 Timothy 1:8-9; 1 John 3:4.

6

Using the Law and the prophets are definitely the necessary tools for reaching the proud. The Way of the Master has emphasized the prophets in a few books, but I haven't seen much detail about prophecy in actual one-to-one witnessing or open-air preaching. Is it best not to get into Bible prophecy, as Peter did in Acts 2, to target the intellect for people who don't believe that the Bible is true?

Prophecy addresses the intellect. The Law addresses the conscience. I often speak about how the words of Jesus parallel history before it came into being, and how Matthew 24 and Luke 21 are proofs of the inspiration of Scripture. However, I am quick to move from there to the Law. That's where the rubber meets the road—the cross makes no sense without the knowledge of sin.

7

Why was the Law omitted in evangelism at the turn of the last century? What caused preachers to stop using it?

It's baffling why any army would leave its greatest weapon in the barracks and go into the battle armed with a feather duster. This, however, has revealed the subtlety of the enemy and reminds us to be tenacious in our use of the Law to bring the knowledge of sin.

8

When I talk with pastors about The Way of the Master and having an evangelism team in the church, their common question is, "How successful are your evangelistic efforts?" Because we are not pushing for conversions, we don't have those numbers to give. Also, a majority of people we witness to are not from our hometown, so we'll never see them walk into our church. So what do we point to as evidence of our efforts? Today's seeker-friendly church keeps requesting, "Show me the numbers!"

I am always amazed at the results pointed to by modern evangelism. They report how many were saved under their preaching, but how did they get access to the Book of Life? Making a "decision," walking an aisle or raising a hand do not indicate whether someone truly repents and trusts in the Savior. I have no idea how many God may have saved through my planting of seeds. The fact that I have planted the good seed of the Word of God is evangelistic "success." The rest is up to God. Read 1 Corinthians 15:58 over and over. Never be discouraged. Your labor isn't in vain.

9

In your opinion, what is the primary reason why people don't want to use this method of evangelism, other than fear of rejection?

That is a mystery to me. Why would anyone want to fish with a net that is full of holes, when God has provided a perfect net to catch men? My only explanation is that there is a spiritual blindness. I have lost count of the number of people who have said they heard the teaching a second time and then suddenly "got it"! It was as though a light switched on in their head.

10

If someone understands that these truths are biblical and approves of the method but replies, "It's not for me," how should we respond? Is this the only biblical method?

The question is simply, "Is it biblical?" Did Jesus use it? Did the disciples use it? Did the Early Church use it? If so, there should be no argument. If it is indeed the God-given key to reaching the lost, why wouldn't we use it? For further reading on the biblical basis for this teaching, we have a book on this subject called *What Did Jesus Do?*

11

I have a dear sister in Christ who believes that fear of eternal damnation does not lead one to a long-term relationship with God. How do you reason with Christians who love God but believe it is wrong to discuss sin with unbelievers?

This philosophy makes no sense if you follow her line of reasoning. Jesus was confrontational. He talked about sin. He spoke to the woman at the well (see John 4) about the fact that she was committing adultery. Study Paul's words in Romans 2, or the Books of James, Peter or Jude. The cold, hard fact is that if people die in their sins, they will end up in hell forever. If we love them, we will work with the Holy Spirit to do everything we can to awaken them to their danger. The Bible says that they are enemies of God and under His wrath, so saying, "God loves you" will only confuse them. Unless they repent, they will perish, and they won't repent if they think that they are morally good.

Another point is, how do you show sinners that God loves them? Do you point to their health or wealth? If that's the criteria, millionaires are more loved than most of us, and healthy people are more loved than those who are gravely ill. The only biblical way to convince sinners that God loves them is to point to the cross. In almost every place in Scripture where God's love is mentioned, it is in correlation to the cross: "In this is love, not that we loved God, but that He loved us and sent His Son to be a propitiation for our sins" (1 John 4:10, emphasis added). "For God so loved the world that He gave His only begotten Son" (John 3:16, emphasis added). "God demonstrates His own love toward us, in that while we were still sinners, Christ died for us" (Romans 5:8, emphasis added).

12

When I use the Law as I witness to people, I sometimes wonder if they have watched *The Way of the Master* and will recognize the "technique" when I go through the Commandments with them. How can we avoid becoming cookie-cutter evangelists, each with the same technique?

It was never my intention to have people do exactly what I do when sharing the gospel. So, just follow the biblical principle of Law to the proud and grace to the humble and let your own personality and ingenuity come through when you witness. Don't be too concerned with people's criticisms; our praise should be from God, not from men. I have had people say, "I've seen this on television," but I find that more of a help than a hindrance.

13

What if someone says they don't believe we will be judged by the Ten Commandments?

The Bible makes it clear that there will be a Day of Judgment. The Scriptures warn, "Though they join forces, the wicked will not go unpunished" (Proverbs 11:21). However, there are those who question the standard of judgment—will it be the Ten Commandments—the moral Law? Some say that it will rather be the words of Jesus that will judge mankind. This belief is based on John 12:48: "He who rejects Me, and does not receive My words, has that which judges him—the word that I have spoken will judge him in the last day."

Humanity will be judged by the words of Jesus, but remember that the Scriptures say that the Lord would "magnify the law, and make it honourable" (Isaiah 42:21, *KJV*). This was the essence of the teaching ministry of the Messiah. The religious leaders had twisted the Law and demeaned it so that its original intent was lost. But Jesus magnified it. He showed them that lust was adultery, and that anger without cause violated its holy precepts. He reminded them that not one jot or tittle of the Law would fail.

When Paul preached on Mars Hill, recorded in Acts 17, he warned the idolatrous Athenians that God would judge the world "in righteousness" (v. 31). They had violated the First and Second of the Ten Commandments, and he therefore warned them that God was not "shaped by art and man's devising" (v. 29). The "righteousness" of which he spoke is the righteousness which is of the Law: "For as many as have sinned without law will also perish without law, and as many as have sinned in the law *will be judged by the law*" (Romans 2:12, emphasis added). James 2:12 also warns that the moral Law will be the standard of judgment: "So speak and so do as those who will be judged by the law of liberty."

Those who may be tempted to say that the "law of liberty" isn't the moral Law, but "the law of Christ," should look at the context. The preceding verse says: "For He who said, '*Do not commit adultery*' [7th Commandment], also said, '*Do not murder*' [8th Commandment]. Now if you do not commit adultery, but you do murder, you have become a transgressor of the law" (James 2:11, emphasis added).

14

Why is there so much opposition among evangelicals concerning The Way of the Master? How do we approach this problem?

It is spiritual, so make sure that you fight it spiritually—with prayer, love and self-control.

15

What about the role of your testimony in witnessing? Isn't it helpful to tell others what Christ has done in your own life as part of your sharing?

Absolutely. If I remember rightly, the apostle Paul shared his personal testimony three times in the Book of Acts. Just make sure you weave the Law into your testimony. Too often we give the impression that we weren't happy, that there was something missing in our lives, until we found Jesus. Instead, explain how you came to see that you were condemned under the Law, headed for hell, and how God's grace saved you through the cross.

HANDLING A WITNESSING ENCOUNTER

I have known what it is to use up all my ammunition, and then I have, as it were, rammed myself into the great gospel gun and fired myself at the hearers—all my experience of God's goodness, all my consciousness of sin, and all my sense of the power of the gospel.

CHARLES SPURGEON

1

A Catholic fellow who was well versed in evangelical doctrine kept asking me what I believed about nonessential doctrines and whether I knew that other evangelicals would disagree with me. If I didn't support a particular doctrine, he tried to debate me on it, even though he didn't believe it himself. I tried going through the Law, but we never got anywhere—we just ended up with a lengthy discussion on evangelical differences. What do you do when the person you're witnessing to tries to turn the conversation into a debate?

I would be firm with someone like this and say, "How about I give you two minutes to speak, without interruption, and then you give me two minutes." Make sure he agrees to do this, and then hold him to his word and take him through the Commandments.

2

What do you do when someone still doesn't see his sin, even after being taken through the Ten Commandments? I talked to one person who was convinced that lust really wasn't a violation of the Ten Commandments.

If a man rapes a woman and doesn't think that rape is a violation of man's law, it doesn't change the fact that it is. Here is proof that lust is a violation of the Ten Commandments: "You have heard that it was said to those of old, 'You shall not commit adultery' [Seventh Commandment]. But I say to you that whoever looks at a woman to lust for her has already committed adultery with her in his heart" (Matthew 5:27-28). So there you have it from the highest authority on earth—the Word of the living God.

If you have the word of a king or a president, you have it on great authority. But this comes from the authority of the Word of God Himself. So, make sure that you quote the verse and don't just refer to it. Jesus quoted the Old Testament word for word when He was tempted by the devil. God's Word doesn't return void. It is quick and powerful and cuts through to the marrow of a sinner's bones (see Hebrews 4:12), so quote it when you share the gospel.

Another way to strengthen the lust argument is to reason about it. Tell the sinner that "lust" is pornography of the mind. Ask him if he thinks child porn okay. The odds are he will say that it's morally wrong. That's his moral standard. God's standard is higher than his, and He says that lust for anyone other than your spouse is morally wrong.

Also, never forget that you have the sinner's conscience on your side. It bears witness with the Law (see Romans 2:15), and of course you have the help of God Himself, who promises that the Holy Spirit will convict of sin. So plant the seed and trust that God will faithfully cause it to grow.

3

What if someone doesn't believe that "taking God's name in vain" is a sin?

The Greek word used for "blasphemy" is *blasphemia. Blas* means "speech," and *phemia* means "against God or sacred persons or things." Any speech against God is blasphemy. The apostle Paul considered himself a blasphemer before his conversion (see 1 Timothy 1:13) because he spoke against Jesus of Nazareth. But God's name is so holy that even using His name without due respect is considered blasphemy. People often use it casually and without meaning, as "just an expression," which God clearly condemns. How much more evil then is it to use His name as a cuss word to express disgust?

Another argument that may come up is that the Seventh Commandment refers only to adultery, not fornication (sex before marriage). That's not true. First Timothy 1:8-10 makes it clear that the Law condemns not only fornicators but also homosexuals.

Finally, some people point out that the Ninth Commandment says, "You shall not *bear false witness*" (Exodus 20:16). They maintain that this refers solely to giving false witness *in a court of law*, and therefore doesn't include everyday lying. Another untruth. First Timothy 1:8-10 also says that the Law was made for liars. So, as much as the world would like to do away with the Law, or at least water it down, it's immutable. It's not going away, and it will be the unbending standard of judgment on the day when God judges the hearts of men and women (see Romans 2:12).

4

What if someone says the only Commandment he has ever broken is the one about lying? Do you press for more by going back over the Commandments, or do you just go with that single once-in-a-lifetime sin?

Committing even one sin, one time, is enough to send him to hell (see James 2:10). But we know that every person has a multitude of sins. For starters, he has failed to love God with all of his heart, soul, mind and strength. He has dishonored his parents' good name by being a liar. Besides that, you can't trust anything he says, because he is a self-admitted liar. However, I usually say, "There's bad news. *All* liars will have their part in the lake of fire" (see Rev. 21:8). I explain that lying is very serious to God. The Bible says that "lying lips are an abomination to the LORD" (Proverbs 12:22).

5

What if someone says that if God is good, He must be all-forgiving? Someone asked me, "If God is all-forgiving and merciful, why do I need to do anything about my so-called sin? He'll forgive everyone no matter what, so why worry about a hell?"

God is not "all-forgiving." He is just and holy. He will by no means clear the guilty (see Numbers 14:18), and any who are found guilty on Judgment Day will come under His terrible wrath. The "all-forgiving" god is an idol, so use the Law to reveal the holiness of God to your hearers.

6

How do you respond to someone who says he doesn't care if he's going to hell?

That person doesn't really believe that he's going there. No one in his right mind would want to go to hell, so you have to do your best to show him there is such a place and God is right and just to send him there.

I often ask those who say they don't care: Have you ever been in a dentist chair and had the drill hit a nerve? Most have. I then ask if they enjoyed the experience. Most didn't. Then I talk about what the Bible says hell is like, and I take them through the Law to show that they are heading there.

If you have taken them through the Law and they are still unconcerned, ask if they would sell an eye for a million dollars. Most won't. They value their eyes; they are above price. So how much more should they value the soul that looks out of those eyes? Don't be afraid to plead with the person.

7

What do you do when you've gone through the Law with someone and explained how Jesus paid his fine, but he or she is still unimpressed? What do you do when the person doesn't grasp the gravity of the situation?

Remember that God resists the proud and gives grace to the humble (see James 4:6), so don't feel compelled to give the Good News to a proud, self-righteous sinner. That person is only ready for grace if he or she has been humbled by the Law. Perhaps you didn't open up the Law and stir the conscience enough. So, soberly go through the Commandments again and warn the person again, and then leave it in the hands of God. Pray that He brings conviction of sin.

Also keep in mind that different personalities react differently. Some people don't like to show their feelings. Others are a little dense. You can tell them that the plate is hot, but they remain unconvinced until they touch it. So don't go by your feelings. If you plant a garden, have confidence in the seed, water it as regularly as you can, then trust God to make the seeds grow.

8

If you have walked through the WDJD outline of biblical evangelism and the person is not humble but rather still in their pride and self-righteousness, do you stop there or do you present grace (Christ crucified) so that he or she has the full gospel to consider? I'm thinking of Jesus' admonition in Matthew 7:6, "Do not give what is holy to the dogs; nor cast your pearls before swine, lest they trample them under their feet, and turn and tear you in pieces."

If they are proud, self-righteous and contentious, leave the Law on them. Then pray that they will humble themselves and be receptive to the message of grace. This is what Jesus did with the rich young ruler. He loved him, but He let him go without hearing of the love of God. Perhaps you could offer the person a tract and ask him to read it later.

9

What if some people don't feel guilty over their sins because of their culture?

There's no need to even go near an issue like polygamy. Instead, use the Law to produce enough guilt for him to see his need of God's mercy. When he sees that he's a liar, a thief, an adulterer and so forth and trusts in the Savior, God Himself will, in time, convict him of any other cultural sins.

10

What does it mean to have a "seared" conscience? Does it mean that the person is unreachable?

A "seared" conscience doesn't necessarily mean a *dead* conscience. Rather, it is one that is deadened on the outside. Sin sears the conscience until its muffled voice is no longer heard. This is a tragedy, because the conscience is the voice of warning. Those who delight in sin because they have dulled their conscience are like a man who removes the batteries from his smoke detector because he doesn't want to be bothered by its alarm.

To awaken a deadened conscience, simply take the person through the Law. Address the conscience directly by saying, "You *know* it's wrong to lie, steal, commit adultery." As you do so, the conscience will confirm the truth of the Commandments.

11

How should I respond to someone who says, "Your religion is all about faith"?

Most of life is about faith. We put our faith in pilots when we trust them with our lives. Marriage is built on faith. So are business partnerships. So is friendship. I can't be mutual friends with someone I don't trust. We exercise faith when we eat food prepared by another person; we trust our weight to a chair when we sit in it. We have faith in history books, weather forecasters and politicians (well, maybe not). We place our faith in these items, and people, based on what we believe is evidence that they are trustworthy.

However, the questioner's statement implies that Christians are living by a naïve, blind faith based on something we can't see, when the opposite is the case. Our faith is rational and reasonable, based on credible, verifiable, historical evidence. The God who created us has given us all the evidence we need to come to know Him. You may want to recommend that atheists read the book *How to Know God Exists*. It's also important to explain the difference between believing something (the Bible), and trusting Someone (Jesus Christ).

12

How can I prove that Christianity is the only way to get to God?

All religions are manmade and are rooted in self-righteousness. Their followers are ignorant of God's righteousness (which comes through the Law), and because of that ignorance, they go about to establish their own righteousness. Only in Christianity is the believer given the righteousness of God through faith in Jesus Christ.

For more details, you may want to read our popular booklet called *Why Christianity?* It shows how the Christian faith is head and shoulders (understatement) above every other religion, and it does so without being condescending. It makes the reason for the cross make sense. According to one reviewer, "It is the best explanation of the gospel I've ever read." You can find them on our website, www.WayOfTheMaster.com, under "booklets."

13

How would you respond if someone asks, "How do you know your belief in Christianity is right?"

If someone sincerely asks this question, then confine him or her under the Law and show that person that it isn't a question of being "right." It's rather a question of having no alternative to the dilemma created by the Law. When a sinner sees sin in its true light, no self-righteous religion is going to satisfy the wrath of God against sin. The only salvation from death and hell is the one that God provided in Jesus Christ. The Law throws a man into a burning desert. He is about to die of thirst when he looks up and sees that God is offering him a glass of cool, clear water in the gospel. There is no alternative to the grace of God in Christ.

14

Some people argue that I believe Christianity only because I was raised in a Christian culture. When someone says, "If you had grown up in a different country or culture, you would believe in their religion," how should I respond?

This sounds complex, but actually it is quite simple. It is true that children do tend to adopt the religion they learned about from their parents. In all other religions, one automatically becomes a follower by birth, by being baptized as an infant or by observing certain religious practices.

But one becomes a Christian only by truly repenting of his sins and placing his trust in Jesus Christ alone for his salvation. It is entirely a work of God, and God will save whom He will no matter where they are located. God knows those whose hearts are truly seeking Him, and He ensures that they hear the gospel. He can reveal Himself to people even in the midst of Hindu, Muslim or animist cultures, so they can put their trust in the Savior. Always remember that believing something doesn't necessarily make it true. Only Christianity is backed up by objective, historical, archaeological and experiential evidence to verify that it is true.

15

How do I witness to someone who insists that God does not love her and who has decided to give her life to Satan?

She already belongs to Satan. Tell her that. He's her god. He has blinded her mind. He's the spirit that works in the children of disobedience. He came to steal, kill, and destroy (see John 10:10), and he is her father. Don't tell her that God loves her. Keep the good wine until last. Tell her that God is angry at her because of her sin, and that's something she won't understand until you apply the Law to her conscience. If you leave the Law out of the equation, she will have a victim mentality, when she should see herself as a criminal.

16

Where does the love of God come in when you're dealing with those who have the wrath of God upon them?

Pay attention to what the person you're witnessing to is saying. The mouth speaks out of the abundance of the heart (see Luke 6:45). Is the person humble? Is he contrite? Is he sober in attitude? Or is he proud, self-righteous, trying to justify himself? The general rule is "Law to the proud, grace to the humble." You will have to make that call yourself as to when to bring in the cross. Only when people understand that they justly deserve God's wrath will His love displayed on the cross make sense.

17

How do you answer someone who says, "If God loves me so much, why are you telling me that instead of Him? Why do I have to read about it? How come God doesn't tell me Himself with His own voice?"

First, I would never speak of the love of God until I had opened up the Law and showed our sinful condition. The love of God isn't fully understood until the cross is understood. And the cross won't make much sense until there is a knowledge of sin. The more heinous the crime, the greater the mercy of the judge to acquit the criminal. The Law is what magnifies the love of God.

Besides, God did manifest Himself to Israel once, and it was so terrifying they thought they were going to die (see Exodus 20:18-20). When God spoke to Jesus once, the Scriptures say that the people thought that it thundered (see John 12:27-29). The fact is that God has chosen the foolishness of preaching to save those who believe. If the person wants God to speak further to him personally, he will have to read the Bible. We speak to God in prayer, and He speaks to us through His Word, and His Word tells us that He proved His love for us through the cross.

18

I have a friend who is an atheist. I asked what kept her from believing in God, and she said that she can't imagine a being who cares about all the problems and wishes of everyone on earth. She said it's not logical. How can I explain to her about God's love for us in a way that she would understand?

Her concept of God is erroneous. He is not some sort of divine butler who is here to care for "all our problems and wishes." That may have been the picture painted for her by modern preachers, and so the god she can't believe in is an idol. It's no wonder she has no faith in it. It doesn't exist.

The way to show her God's love and His incredible, omnipotent power is to take her through the Commandments. Show her that she is a desperate criminal in the sight of a holy God, and she is in danger of eternal damnation in a terrible place called hell. That will help her to see that God is not a cosmic Santa Claus whose power is limited, but a just judge who is willing to save her if she will repent. Don't be concerned if she maintains that she doesn't believe in God. Tell her that she has to face Him anyway. Once she is born again and understands a little of God's absolute magnificence, then she will have no trouble believing that He can do anything.

19

When I ask someone if he or she is saved and that person sarcastically says, "Saved from what?" What is the proper response?

The person almost has a right to be sarcastic (what Shakespeare called "the lowest form of wit"). As Christians, we should be careful when we use words like "saved," because they make no sense to an unbeliever. We put up signs that say things like "Jesus saves" and wonder why the world asks which bank He saves at. I would never ask a person if he is saved. I find that the best way to witness is to first begin in the natural realm and then ask what they think happens after someone dies: "What's on the other side?"

20

In the Philippines, our culture (Filipino and Chinese) emphasizes respect for elders. How can we go through the Ten Commandments or even ask, "Would you consider yourself to be a good person?" or talk about death and hell without sounding disrespectful? Older Chinese people dislike hearing about death, so how could I share the gospel with them?

I think almost all of us feel very uncomfortable witnessing to elderly people we love and respect. But that's the point—if we love and respect them, we will talk to them. The reason they don't like talking about death is that they are afraid of dying (see Hebrews 2:14-15)—something that's true for all of us. You have found the answer for them, and if you care about them you will take courage and speak to them. The fear dissipates once you begin the conversation.

Just ask, "What do you think happens after someone dies?" That will let you know if you have a green or red light. If you are afraid that it will look as though you are pointing a finger, use your testimony when you share the gospel—for example, "I didn't realize that lying lips were an abomination to the Lord and that all liars will end up in the lake of fire."

21

When someone says, "Well, I'm not perfect," or, "No one is perfect," how do you respond biblically in light of Matthew 5:48?

Agree with the person. What he is seeking to do is justify his sinful heart by spreading the blame around all of humanity and at the same time inferring that the standard God requires is too high. Play his game. Say, "That's right; you are not perfect. You are a self-admitted liar and thief, and you have to stand before a perfect God whose Law you have violated and give an account of your actions. What are you going to say? You can't justify yourself. And you are right about no one being perfect. We have all sinned, and we are all heading for hell."

The person's words reveal a subtle form of self-righteousness, and you have to chop that out with the sharp ax of the Law. So cut deep and get it all out. You want to bring him to a point of saying, "*I* have sinned against God." His sin is personal. Study Paul's use of the Law in Romans 2:21-23. He stirred the conscience and he made it personal. Nathan did the same thing with David when he told him, "You are the man!" Study the opening verses of Psalm 51 to see how personal David knew his transgression was—knowledge that came from the prophet's rebuke. Count the number of David's references to himself and his personal guilt. Also notice that he calls what he did "evil," not just being "imperfect":

> Have mercy upon me, O God, according to Your lovingkindness; according to the multitude of Your tender mercies, blot out my transgressions. Wash me thoroughly from my iniquity, and cleanse me from my sin. For I acknowledge my transgressions, and my sin is always before me. Against You, You only, have I sinned, and done this evil in Your sight—that You may be found just when You speak, and blameless when You judge (Psalm 51:1-4).

22

I'm sometimes asked, "What about the people who have never heard of Jesus Christ—are you saying that they are all going to hell?" That's been a very frequent and difficult one for me. How would you respond?

The inference is that the people who have never heard the gospel are basically good people, and that God would be unjust to send them to hell. So, tell the questioner that they will be fine—if they are good people. However, in God's eyes, a good person is one who is morally perfect in thought, word and deed. That means that they will be in trouble with God if they have committed murder (hated anyone), adultery (lusted), theft (taken anything), or if they have lied. God will do what is right and just and will punish wrongdoing no matter where it's found. If they have broken even one Law, they will get what's coming to them. (This is dealt with in the first three chapters of the Book of Romans.) That's why we send missionaries to these people—so they can be saved from their sins through faith in Jesus. Then say, "Now, let's get back to you . . ."

WITNESSING TO CERTAIN GROUPS

What can be wiser than in the highest sense to bless our fellow men—to snatch a soul from the gulf that yawns, to lift it up to the Heaven that glorifies, to deliver an immortal from the thralldom of Satan, and to bring him into the liberty of Christ.

CHARLES SPURGEON

1

If management tells us not to witness at work anymore, are we supposed to stop sharing our faith? How can we reach our coworkers with the gospel?

If your boss forbids it, don't do it on work time. Instead, keep a pile of million-dollar bill tracts or some other tract on your desk, but don't give them out. If someone asks for one, let them take it. Show your faith by your works—let love shine. Give your coworkers small gifts (but not for the opposite sex—unless it's a gift from you and your spouse, with a card that says so).

I would also invite unsaved coworkers out to lunch (again, not the opposite sex), and witness to them there. Just ask for their thoughts on what happens after death. That will let you know if they are open to the gospel. If you detect contention, apologize and instead use closet prayer. Management can't stop you from praying, so determine that the more they stop you from witnessing, the more you are going to pray. Make a list of workers and uphold them before God, asking for divine openings to witness.

2

I became a believer about five months ago. My family is having a hard time dealing with that, just as I am having a hard time dealing with the fact that they are not saved. I have tried to witness to them, but they are becoming tired of listening. How can I effectively witness to my family members?

I know the frustration of having witnessed to friends and family, but they are still unconcerned about their salvation. You can't preach to them every time you see them; that would kill the relationship. It drives me crazy, though, that they could be snatched into hell forever, and they don't really care.

Deal with your concerns for them in the prayer closet. Pray for them and then love them, not with words but with actions. Instead of preaching, continue to show them your faith by your works. Buy gifts when it's not Christmas or a birthday. Mow lawns, wash dishes and clean cars. Be rich in good works so they can see that your faith is genuine. Put yourself in their position. As far as they are concerned, you have joined some religious cult. Prove them wrong by being sincerely loving, kind and very down-to-earth. Then witness to them only if they bring up the subject. But make sure that you pray for the opportunity to speak, and be watchful for it. In the meantime, witness to other Christians' unsaved loved ones, and trust that God will send some faithful Christian witness to yours.

3

My mother is hardened toward the gospel and rarely lets me get a word in edgewise when it comes to religion or politics. She appears to think that most Christians—with the exception of her best friend—are hypocrites, including me. What is the best way to witness to her?

Pray that her best friend witnesses to her. People often feel very uncomfortable speaking about spiritual things with a relative, but they will open up to a friend or stranger. Why would your own mother think that you are a hypocrite? Make sure your life is without hypocrisy. Ask her what has caused her to think like that, and apologize if necessary. Then strive to honor and love her unconditionally.

4

I am trying to share my faith with my father, with whom I only communicate through email, and every time I try he either doesn't respond or gets angry. Can you give me any advice on how to make him understand when I can't talk to him face-to-face or have an actual conversation with him?

Make sure you are using the Law before grace. If he won't listen to you, you have other means of helping him. Pray for him and openly show that you love him. Do anything you can to build a relationship with him. If someone sends you a humorous email, forward it to him.

Send him gifts out of the blue. When you pray, believe that God will save him. That means no doubts, no fears, no worries. It means thanking God for His kindness in drawing your dad to Himself. Don't get caught up on issues of election; leave that up to God. You may also want to check out the online evangelistic tools on our website (www.livingwaters.com) under "Free Evangelism Resources."

5

I have a born-again daughter who has converted to Catholicism (her boyfriend is Catholic). I love her no matter what, but what can I say? Should I bring up the Ten Commandments?

I know this is painful to hear, but I wouldn't be too quick to say that your daughter is born-again. If Jesus Christ is her Lord and Savior, she will not only love the truth, but she will never be unequally yoked with an unbeliever. Roman Catholicism rests on a foundation of works as a means of salvation. It denies that we are saved by grace alone through faith alone, apart from works. If works are involved, then salvation isn't the gift of God (see Ephesians 2:8-9).

Only the self-righteous trust in works, so what you must do is chop down the roots of that poisonous tree. The only biblical and therefore effective means of doing that is to go through the Commandments. Put your daughter on the witness stand. Show her that she is a guilty criminal and that her good works are an attempt to bribe the Judge of the Universe. Use the Law as a schoolmaster to bring her to Christ. Drive her to the cross. When she repents and trusts in Jesus alone for her salvation, the Holy Spirit will then lead her into all truth. In the meantime, continue to pray for and love her as much as you can.

6

What's the best way to witness to someone who is much older than me?

People who have been on this earth a while and who haven't come to faith are usually steeped in self-righteousness, and it is awkward for younger people to speak to them because we tend to respect those who are (much) older than us. It may therefore be easier to witness in the first person. Instead of asking, "Have you ever lusted after someone?" you can say, "I didn't realize that God considered lust to be adultery, and hatred to be the same as murder." That way, it gets the message across but is less accusatory.

7

At what age can you begin to talk to children about salvation?
I've gone through the process a number of times with my four children,
ages six and under, but I also know that abstract reasoning will not begin
until the age of nine or ten. So should I wait to talk to my
children until they're a certain age?

That depends on their maturity. Some children come to Christ at a very young age, but it doesn't happen too often. The biblical thing to do is to train up the child in the way he should go (see Proverbs 22:6). Teach him the Law. Soak him in Scripture. Teach him the fear of the Lord. We have a practical book called *How to Bring Your Children to Christ . . . and Keep Them There*, which you may find very beneficial. It will help you avoid the heartbreaking trap of a false conversion in a child.

8

How do I reach someone who is adamantly atheistic without scaring him away?
I have been trying to talk to this person every chance I get about Jesus and the wonderful
things He can do for us, but I don't seem to be getting anywhere. What can I do?

Listen to "Hell's Best Kept Secret" free on our website to see how unbiblical it is to approach a proud person (which an atheist is) and talk about Jesus and the wonderful things He can do for them. We also have a TV episode called "God Has a Wonderful Plan" that addresses this subject. You can view it free online at www.livingwaters.com (both of these can be found under "free evangelism resources"). Your friend needs the Law. He needs to fear God. These teachings will help you know how to speak to him.

9

How do you witness to people who believe in evolution and don't want to hear about God?

If you are unable to reason with them, there is little else you can do but pray for people who are close-minded. However, if their faith in evolution is strong enough to withstand a challenge—and they are open to considering whether the evidence supports their belief—you could give them the book *Evolution: A Fairytale for Grown-ups* or *How to Know God Exists: Sci-*

entific Proof of God. The evidence presented in these books will give them compelling reasons to doubt their faith in the theory.

10

How do you witness to a Gnostic—someone who believes that God is really evil, the serpent in Eden was really the Holy Spirit, and the knowledge that Jesus taught is what saves a person?

Don't address the character of God at this point. Instead, address the sin of this person by taking him through the Ten Commandments. Show him that he is a wicked criminal and that he has added to his sins by saying that God is evil. Lay it on thick and heavy. This is a terrible sin because it goes against the light of our conscience. We inherently know that God is good by nature; and to say that He is evil is odious.

11

What do you say to people who believe in reincarnation?

Don't get sidetracked into discussing it. I normally ask what they think they will come back as and what they would like to be in the next life. I may ask what they did to merit coming back in this life as a human being, and who is in charge of dealing out all the new bodies . . . is it God? But I do it in a lighthearted way. Then I say, "If there is a place called heaven, do you think that you are good enough to go there?" Then I take them through the Law. During that time I often mention that the Bible says, "It is appointed for men to die once, but after this the judgment" (Hebrews 9:27).

12

I have a Chinese coworker with whom I've shared the gospel. I noticed some "decorations" hanging in his car, which he said were for protection. Do I need to convince him to get rid of those things, or should I wait until he comes to Christ?

I would dig a little further and ask him about what they actually do. Does he think they have any spiritual power? Where does God fit in with all this? Try to talk him out of trusting in them because they more than likely have some sort of negative spiritual power, although I don't believe they can stop him from coming to Christ (which is probably your concern). The Gadarene demoniac was full of demons, but he was still able to fall at the Savior's feet (see Luke 8:26-39). You might want to get a copy of the book *Out of the Comfort Zone*. Chapter 10, "Invisible Realms," could open his eyes. It is frightening.

13

I presented the Law to a Muslim, and he agreed that God had a moral Law and admitted he would be found guilty. However, he said that in Islam, people are punished "for a while" and then sent to Paradise. I kept asking how his fine is paid in the Muslim faith, and he went back to punishment and then release to Paradise. I pointed out from Scripture that hell is forever, not a temporary place of punishment. How would you have responded to this person?

I would take him to civil court and give an example of a criminal who had raped and murdered a number of young girls. Paint the crime as being extremely heinous, because that's what sin is in God's sight. It is obvious that he doesn't see sin as being very serious if it necessitates only temporal punishment. We tend to trivialize crimes against God with words like "fibs" and "white" lies, but the Scriptures tell us that "lying lips are an abomination to the Lord" (Proverbs 12:22). Lying is so serious in God's sight that all liars will have their part in the lake of fire. All you can do is plant the seed of truth and then pray that God makes your words (His truth) come to life in the man's heart.

14

How do you witness to someone who "accepted Christ" as a child but hasn't attended church as an adult and doesn't think he needs to do so?

The person has almost certainly had a false conversion, so you need to speak with him the same way you would speak to any other unsaved person. Don't feel intimidated by the fact that he has made a profession of faith. If it were genuine, he would be obedient to the Word of God. I wouldn't even address the experience. Simply ask for his thoughts on the afterlife and ask whether he thinks he's good enough to go to heaven. If he does, take him through the Law. If he speaks of salvation by grace, and that's what he is trusting in, ask him when he last read his Bible. If he is into the Word daily, tell him that it's important that he get into fellowship with other believers, and then pray that he does. You can't do much more than that.

15

When you ask strangers whether they are Christians and they say they are, but you suspect they may be false converts, how can you arrive at the truth concerning their salvation?

Most people in the United States think they are "Christian." They think a Christian is someone who believes in God, or who isn't of another religious persuasion. So, ask if they have been "born again." If there is the slightest hesitation, be suspicious. Since some people believe they've been "born again" many times, you may want to say something like this (in a very friendly tone): "I love to hear how people come to know the Lord. Would you mind sharing your personal testimony?" Two other probing questions are, "Do you consider yourself to be a good person?" (false converts usually do) and, "When did you last read your Bible?"

16

What do you say to a Christian who has a beer in one hand and a cigarette in the other?

I would ask him when he last read his Bible and if he thinks he's a good person. If he is reading the Word daily and seems to have a good understanding of salvation, I would gently let him know that he should pray about how he presents himself. He should be without reproach, and not even eat meat if it offends a brother (see Romans 14:21). Tell him that what he is doing is offensive to you and it may be a stumbling block to others. He is also defiling his body—the temple of the Holy Spirit—by abusing it with known poisons.

17

How would you witness to someone who has grown up in church and knows who God is and what Christianity means, but says that he has too much fun sinning and will just accept Christ later so he can go to heaven when he dies?

This person lacks a fear of God. As always, this traces itself back to idolatry. As a child, he was probably taught that Jesus is your buddy and the celestial problem solver, and then in church he heard the message of the modern gospel. He needs to have the fear of God put into him. Take him through the Law, speak of future punishment and point out that God may kill him before he makes his decision to "accept" Christ. Put him on the witness stand; show him that he is a devious criminal who is about to be executed and sent to an everlasting and fearful hell.

Do it in love and in gentleness, but reprove and rebuke him, with all longsuffering and doctrine. Tell him what Jesus said in Matthew 7:21-23, and remind him about how God called a man a fool because he put off his salvation and trusted that he had many days ahead of him (see Luke 12:13-21).

18

What do you do when a Christian friend is falling out of the will of God? He knows the Ten Commandments but doesn't see anything wrong with what he is doing and gets angry when I try to talk to him about it.

I assume you are saying that he is willfully getting into sin. This is a sign of a false conversion. I would send a loving letter, saying that you are deeply concerned for him. I would suggest that you first read 1 John 1–3 and Matthew 7.

19

How do you witness to people you know well and who are devoutly religious, yet you still question their salvation? How do you avoid sounding as if you are judging them? I have several friends who are very religious, but I think they are trying to earn their salvation by doing good works.

I know that this can be uncomfortable. However, think about how you would feel if one of these friends was killed in a car accident tonight. If you care about that person, you must say something. So many people we know now as being on fire, God-loving, evangelizing Christians were once in the category of either being religious or false converts, and they are eternally grateful that someone brought them the true gospel.

The "religious" are those who are trusting in their own efforts to obtain salvation, and there are millions in this category. But the false converts are those who are just as deceived. They are those who name the name of Christ, profess a new-birth experience but don't have the things that accompany salvation. There is no evidence that they are truly saved. There are millions of false converts also. These categories of people need to be awakened (with God's help), by those who care enough to risk offending them.

Both religious people and false converts can usually be traced back to idolatry. These people don't have an understanding of God's nature. They therefore lack the fear of God and of the truth of salvation by grace alone though faith alone. They are self-righteous. So how do you handle this?

Simply say, "Dave, can I ask you an important question? Do you consider yourself to be a good person?" That will reveal whether he is trusting in his own righteousness or in the cross. It will show you if he understands the gravity of sin. If he says that he is a good person, take him through the Commandments. If he admits his sins but says that he is trusting in Jesus for his salvation, say, "But, Dave, you told me that you think that you are a good person, when Jesus said there is none good but God" (see Mark 10:18).

Ask him if he is reading his Bible *every* day. The odds are that he isn't. It may be every second or third day, or once a week, or never. Ask him how he would rate his walk with the Lord, on a scale of 1 to 10. Tell him that it should be 10 for every one of us. We are to love the Lord our God with all of our heart, soul, mind and strength (see Mark 12:30).

Then point out that Jesus said many will say to Him, "Lord, Lord," on the Day of Judgment, and He will say, "I never knew you; depart from Me, you who practice lawlessness!"(see Matthew 7:21-23). Talk to him about the reality of false conversion and the importance of manifesting the fruit of repentance. Tell him there is nothing more important than his eternal salvation. Then you could perhaps pray with him, encouraging him to make his calling and election sure. The very fact that you have taken him through the Law will bring a sense of sobriety to him about sin (if he is honest of heart). Then keep him in prayer. Of course, it goes without saying that you would use a very loving and concerned tone as you speak with him.

Another approach would be to tell him, "I just listened to an alarming message about the reality of false conversion. Have you ever thought about that—how you can know whether you're truly saved?" Then give him a copy of the message "True & False Conversions" on CD.

20

How do I share the Law with someone whom I have already shared the modern gospel?

If the person is still open to listening, you could earnestly say, "I realize our previous conversations may not have made much sense. Can I share something that will help it be more understandable?"

21

How do you witness to Mormons?

It is very easy to become caught up in arguing about the error of Mormonism. Mormons are ready to defend their religion; they know how to defuse and divert the average Christian's arguments. The key to reaching them is to uncover what they are trusting in for their salvation. They believe that grace isn't enough to save them, so they have to add to the grace of God to be saved. Calvary wasn't enough. This error comes from a wrong concept of God's nature, and therefore a wrong concept of sin. So try saying this to any of the cults: "I have a knife in my back and three minutes to live. My life is draining from my body. What do I have to do to enter the kingdom of God?"

Those who are in cults will usually tell you that you will have to do something to be saved, revealing that the salvation they offer is works based. From there, simply ask the person if he thinks that he is a good person. If he does, take him through the Law and show him that he has sinned against God and that the only thing that can save him is God's mercy. The right use of the Law will put *earned* salvation so far from him that mercy can be his only option. Any works on his part are an attempt to bribe the Judge of the Universe, and God will not be bribed on Judgment Day.

For more details, we have episodes on how to reach Jehovah's Witnesses and Mormons in the third season of *The Way of the Master*. You may like to watch those DVDs.

22

As a pastor, I preach at funerals for the unsaved on a regular basis. While I never comment on the eternal destiny of the deceased, I always preach the gospel plainly and use the Law. Is it advisable to do this? Do you use the Law in the same way as you would with anyone?

It is advisable to share the gospel whenever and wherever we can. You are wise not to comment on any person's eternal destiny. We are usually not privy to conversations sinners have with the Lord in the last moments of life. I say "usually," because we were allowed to hear what was whispered between one repentant thief on a cross and Jesus. God only knows how many sinners say, "Lord, remember me," and Jesus hears them. When the unsaved lose a loved one, they are often open, perhaps for the first time in their lives, to the questions of eternity. So preach to them as though it was your last sermon, and as though it was your audience's last day on earth.

23

An old high school friend called me about the death of his brother, a devout Catholic who was killed in a motorcycle accident while drunk. When he asked me to pray for his brother's soul in purgatory, I said that I couldn't pray for his brother but that I could pray for him. He became angry and said his brother was trapped in purgatory and needed our prayers to get him out. I told him this wasn't biblical at all and that our souls go to either heaven or hell (no purgatory). As I explained that Jesus died for us so we wouldn't have to go to hell and started witnessing with the Law and grace, he ended the conversation and I never heard from him again.
So, how do you respond to a devout Catholic whose loved one has died unsaved?

I admire your love and courage. You did the right thing; so don't be discouraged. Make sure you attempt to stay in contact with your friend. I once had to do something similar with my Catholic aunt (not quite as dramatic as your situation). She said that she had been praying to her dead husband. I told her that he wasn't omniscient and that she should never speak to the dead. It was very awkward for me, but I had to tell her the truth even though it might be offensive to her. The next day she gave me a check for $1,000, out of the blue. I was very surprised, but delighted, because we had just pulled our three kids out of secular school and were putting them into a Christian school, and the money covered the costs. You didn't get a check from an aunt, but I am sure you have your Father's smile.

24

I've found that many of the homeless in our city have been greatly affected by drugs and other things, which has caused their minds to be permanently damaged.
How do I get through to people like this and those with slight mental illnesses?

Keep the gospel very simple. Patiently explain it until the person understands the issues, and then have confidence in God and in the power of the gospel. Obviously, pray with and for the person. Always remember this great truth: With God, nothing is impossible (see Matthew 19:26). There are plenty of Christians who can testify that it was only upon conversion that God gave them a sound mind.

25

Is there ever a time when you think someone isn't worth approaching because they are inappropriately attired or are very drunk? Although we care, and we don't want anyone to go to hell, we also don't want to get ourselves into a bad situation.

I have found that the people with the meanest-looking tattoos and hooks through their nose are often the friendliest. Few others approach them because they look scary, so when someone does approach, it surprises them. When I see people wearing filthy T-shirts with disgusting words on them, my initial reaction is to despise them. Instead, I approach them and am almost always delighted by what I find. Try it.

Regarding drunks, it really depends on how drunk they are. You have to take each case on its own merit. Some drunks get angry, so you are wise to be careful with them.

26

How do you deal with demon-possessed people when you are witnessing to them?

Demonic possession may be much more prevalent than most of us assume. The Bible tells us, "And you He made alive, who were dead in trespasses and sins, in which you once walked according to the course of this world, *according to the prince of the power of the air, the spirit who now works in the sons of disobedience*, among whom also we all once conducted ourselves in the lusts of our flesh, fulfilling the desires of the flesh and of the mind, and were by nature children of wrath, just as the others" (Ephesians 2:1-3, emphasis added). There is a spirit that works in the unsaved, and now and then it is obvious that someone is demonically possessed. The way to deal with them is to do so very gently. Ask the person for his name. Jesus did this. If the individual is spilling over with demons, he (they) may give you a strange demonic name. If he gives you what sounds like his real name, use it as you speak to him. People are less likely to attack you if you use their name when speaking to them. Also, keep in mind that demons cannot stop someone from coming to Christ. Look at Scripture:

Then they came to the other side of the sea, to the country of the Gadarenes. And when He had come out of the boat, immediately there met Him out of the tombs a man with an unclean spirit, who had his dwelling among the tombs; and no one could bind him, not even with chains, because he had often been bound with shackles and chains. And the chains had been pulled apart by him, and the shackles broken in pieces; neither could anyone tame him. And always, night and day, he was in the mountains and in the tombs, crying out and cutting himself with stones.

When he saw Jesus from afar, he ran and worshiped Him. And he cried out with a loud voice and said, "What have I to do with You, Jesus, Son of the Most High God? I implore You by God that You do not torment me." For He said to him, "Come out of the man, unclean spirit!" Then He asked him, "What is your name?" And he answered, saying, "My name is Legion; for we are many" (Mark 5:1-9).

Notice a number of things about this demon-possessed man. He was self-destructive, attracted by death and darkness, tormented and supernaturally strong. But the demons didn't stop him from running to Jesus and worshiping Him. So realize that fact and take the person thoroughly through the Law. He needs to shut the door to sin and not "give place to the devil" (Ephesians 4:27). The key for any person to be free from the demonic realm is to obey the command: "Submit to God. Resist the devil and he will flee from you" (James 4:7).

One other point. Don't chase after the demonic realm. It will more than likely chase after you. Paul was followed by a demon-possessed woman for many days before he lost patience and dealt with her.

OPEN-AIR PREACHING

The open-air speaker's calling is as honorable as it is arduous, as useful as it is laborious.
God alone can sustain you in it, but with Him at your side you will have nothing to fear.
CHARLES SPURGEON

1

Since open-air preaching is mentioned numerous times in Scripture, why does it seem that Christians respond negatively to it? Why have I never heard it preached on?

Unfortunately, there are a few weirdoes who scream at and abuse people as they walk by. These are the ones who make it onto the TV news or are depicted in movies. So you can't blame some people for having a negative attitude toward open-air preaching. However, that's a cross we have to carry.

We don't hear many pastors preaching on the subject—probably because they don't open-air preach. Let's hope and pray that changes. Your example may help. When you stand up and break the sound barrier, never forget, you are in the best of company. Jesus, Paul, Stephen, John Wesley, George Whitefield, and Charles Spurgeon were open-air preachers. There are no better footsteps to follow.

2

What advice would you give someone who has never done open-air preaching but wants to start?

You are needed to "go into the world," so don't listen to your fears. You are going to get them (I still do). They will be so real that they'll make you sweat. But don't listen; just do it.

Have you ever felt the joy of sharing the gospel with someone who is genuinely listening to every word you are saying? Multiply that by 150. That's a good open-air session. There's nothing like it when you have a good heckler and a crowd of people listening to the words of everlasting life.

What is the difference between messages preached in the open air and those preached in a building where people are sitting and attentive?

People in a church building are there willingly and are a captive audience. In the open air, if they don't like what you are saying or you are boring, they leave. Therefore, you need to learn the *skills* of open-air preaching. The analogy of "fishing" for men is so applicable. A good fisherman is a skilled fisherman, and his skill comes by experience. He learns to go where the fish gather. He knows that seagulls gather where the fish are, or that certain seaweed attracts certain fish. He knows how to bait a hook so that it is disguised. He knows when to reel in the fish. These skills come by experience, but for more in-depth teaching to hasten that experience, you can watch our DVD *Open-Air Preaching 4-in-1*.

What are your thoughts on women open-air preaching?

While there is controversy about a woman's role in the church, there is no question about the beneficial nature of having women involved in the task of evangelism. The first evangelists were women. They took the good news of the Resurrection to the disciples, who were cringing behind locked doors. While there are a few who would raise an eyebrow at the thought of a woman preaching in the open air, it is biblical. Here's why. Can you think of any verse that forbids a woman from sharing the gospel with a hell-bound sinner? Of course not. She is commissioned to share her faith. May she witness to two people at once? Of course. How about 20 people at once? How about in an open-air situation where she gets to share the everlasting gospel with 100 sinners?

What is a good way to practice open-air preaching before doing it "live"?

Go over the gospel in your mind until it's second nature—no, until it's first nature. When you are alone, preach it. (In the shower is a great place to preach.) Go through a few anecdotes. Get used to the sound of your own voice. Pretend to engage a heckler. Invite some friends over and practice what you preach.

6

How do you evaluate a good place to station yourself?

Find a place where people gather—beaches, parks, waiting in line—where they're not in a hurry. Select a place that has plenty of foot traffic but away from the noise of the street, a fountain or machinery. It is ideal to have somewhere that will acoustically hold your voice, and where you can be slightly elevated. You shouldn't have problems speaking in public places in the United States; it is your First Amendment right to speak on American soil.

7

How consistently do you stay in one area? Do you constantly try new places?

I will keep going back to an area as long as people will listen to the gospel. This is because it is good for regulars to hear the gospel more than once. You will find that you can befriend these people, and some may even seek you out with questions. Another reason I stick with the same place is because of the old saying, "If it ain't broke, don't fix it." This is also true when you find an effective fishing hole for handing out tracts and witnessing.

8

How do you deal with people that you see again in the same place you had previously open aired?

Try to remember their names and greet them when you see them. If they keep coming back, ask them questions. You may find that you have the blessing of a regular heckler.

9

Do you go by yourself to preach? If not, how many Christians should go with you?

The more laborers there are, the better. A crowd tends to draw a crowd. Just make sure that your helpers don't argue with hecklers or distract your listeners while you're speaking. Tell them to pay attention and not become distracted and start talking to each other. One of the most helpful things your team can do is clap when people answer trivia correctly. Nothing attracts people like applause and laughter. Instruct your helpers to follow those who peel away from the crowd and either give them a tract or try to engage them in conversation.

10

How do you draw a crowd if offering money as a prize doesn't work?

I have tried everything under the sun. Some things work and some don't. The best way I have found to generate interest is to engage someone in conversation. Don't wait until someone heckles you or asks you a question—you ask them. Call on people who stop and listen. Say, "You, sir! Do you think that there's a heaven? Why/why not? Do you think that you are a good person?" Keep at it until his initial shock of being "picked on" wears off. Some of the best hecklers I've had came from me prompting them. So be bold.

11

Do you add any entertainment, such as someone playing a guitar and singing?

If singing would help me get a crowd, I would sing, if I could. I am serious. If I could sing, dance or juggle, I would use that skill for the glory of God. If I could smash wood with my fist, I would use that skill to pull in a crowd. If you have a talent of any sort, give serious consideration to using it to reach the lost.

12

Do you post gospel texts around where you preach?

The Bible tells us that sinners hate the light. So I don't even hold a Bible when I preach. I don't want people to have a prejudicial attitude toward the gospel.

13

What is the most effective way to keep a crowd after revealing the Law?

There are two ways. One is to engage a colorful heckler. By that, I mean one who will speak up and then be quiet while you address his question. The other way is to make sure you preach with passion. People will often listen to you if you speak with conviction.

14

Is contending for the faith and being a bit contentious to draw or maintain the crowd the same thing?

You want to always make sure you are respectful, congenial and uncompromising, but people won't stay and listen to a boring preaching, so you have to be on the edge. Christians sometimes think that it's unloving to speak in such a way, but it is necessary if you want to hold your hearers. If you listened to me share the gospel with people, you would probably notice an obvious gentleness in my tone. However, if you listen to me preach in the open air, it may seem contentious and provocative. This is because if I preached the same way I speak, I would never hold a crowd. It is important in both cases that I am motivated by love, but if I don't keep the preaching "on the edge," I will lose my hearers in minutes (if not seconds).

John Wesley put it this way: "In the streets a man must from beginning to end be intense, and for that very reason he must be condensed and concentrated in his thought and utterance." This "intense" preaching may be misunderstood by those who don't know why the intensity is there. The problem is that when we read the Gospels, we don't see the passion involved in its discourses. When Jesus spoke, there were those in the crowd who hated Him and wanted to kill Him. People undoubtedly called out, accusing Him of blasphemy and other crimes, or they asked Him questions. Without a doubt, the atmosphere would have been electric. That's the atmosphere that holds a crowd's attention. To become passive in the name of love and gentleness will pull the plug out and the electricity will immediately leave.

So be ready, because you may be accused of preaching without love. The accusations almost always come from those brethren who have never preached in the open air. When speaking of open-air preaching, evangelist R. A. Torrey said, "Don't be soft. One of these nice, namby-pamby, sentimental sort of fellows in an open-air meeting, the crowd cannot and will not stand. The temptation to throw a brick or a rotten apple at him is perfectly irresistible, and one can hardly blame the crowd."

15

If police or security officers try to shut us down, how do we effectively deal with them so they'll enable us to continue?

Be very polite. Don't talk about First Amendment rights (that upsets them). Instead ask the officer or security guard if you are breaking the law. If you are, you will gladly leave. If you aren't breaking any law, gently tell them that you are going to keep speaking.

16

How do you get a license to preach on a college campus?

Call the campus, tell them you'd like to come and speak, and ask for their requirements. They may let you speak with or without amplification. You may need some sort of insurance, or they may want to restrict you to a certain area. If there is a Christian organization on the campus that invites you, that usually gets around any red tape.

17

Has there ever been a time doing open-air or even one-to-one when you just didn't know what to say? If you draw a blank while speaking or when someone asks you a question, how do you respond without looking like a complete idiot?

Keep a New Testament with you, and if you freeze up, say, "I would just like to read something to you." Read John 3:16-18 and conclude with, "Thank you for listening." *Just knowing you have that option will dissipate the fear.* If someone asks you a question that you don't know how to answer, simply say, "I'm sorry, I don't know the answer to that." There's nothing wrong with a humble admission. In fact, it may speak more to your hearers than an eloquent answer.

18

Are there certain Scriptures that are more effective or applicable in open-air preaching than in a one-to-one encounter?

They are the same Scriptures you would use in one-to-one. Make sure they are verses that open up the Commandments, and that speak of the cross, repentance and faith.

19

If you don't sense a conviction of sin as you are preaching to a crowd, would you still give the grace part of the sermon?

When open-air preaching, I would. This is because I don't trust my senses. It may seem like a contentious crowd, but there could be one person in that crowd who is listening.

20

What would you say is the most important thing to remember about preaching open air?

We can easily get so caught up in apologetics that we forget to preach the cross. And it's easy to do because it is intellectually stimulating. It's important to always remember that apologetics address the intellect and don't bring conviction of sin. I have seen many open-air situations where the discussion goes on and on and degenerates into an argument. It is the cross that a sinner needs to hear about. Paul said, "For I determined not to know anything among you except Jesus Christ and Him crucified" (1 Corinthians 2:2). In Athens, Paul used apologetics (briefly) as a highway to the cross. That was his destination. Apologetics should be a means to an end, not the end itself. So always keep that in mind, both in preaching and in personal witnessing.

WITNESSING IN GENERAL

We want in the Church of Christ a band of well-trained sharpshooters, who will pick the people out individually and be always on the watch for all who come into the place, not annoying them, but making sure that they do not go away without having had a personal warning, invitation, and exhortation to come to Christ.

CHARLES SPURGEON

1

When Paul spoke in Athens, why did he begin his preaching with creation as opposed to the Law (Acts 17:24)?

In Acts 17:16, we are told that Paul was grieved because the whole city of Athens was given over to idolatry. So, in verses 22-28, he tells his hearers that they had put other gods before the God of creation. He is in essence opening up the First and the Second of the Ten Commandments: "I am the LORD your God. . . . You shall have no other gods before Me. You shall not make for yourself a carved image" (Exodus 20:2-4). Then, in verses 29-31, he rebukes them for their idolatry and preaches repentance and future punishment by the Law ("in righteousness"). So I wouldn't say that he began with creation *as opposed to* the Law. It was what he used to point them to the Law.

Think of how Jesus approached the woman at the well (see John 4). He began to speak to her about water, but then He spoke to her about her violation of the Seventh Commandment. When Nathan was commissioned by God to reprove David for his sins, Nathan began in the natural realm and then pointed out David's transgression: "Why have you despised the commandment of the LORD?" (2 Samuel 12:9).

Although Paul mentioned creation, he didn't stay there for long, because speaking about creation doesn't convict a man of his sins. There is no guilty conscience accusing hearers as long as we speak apologetically. The goal is to use the Law to bring the knowledge of sin.

Many times, I have been caught up in a sword fight about evolution v. atheism, and I've suddenly realized that little progress was being made. These subjects should merely be seen as a means to an end. The end is the preaching of the reality of Judgment Day and the terror of hell—avoided through the cross, repentance and faith. The biblical way there is through the Law. You can see Paul do this as he exposes their idolatry (First and Second Commandments) and preaches future punishment for sin (see Acts 17:29-31).

2

How often do you preach on a subject such as abortion rather than the straightforward "good person" test? How does this work out in terms of audience participation or producing conviction?

We should speak about social sins (pornography, pedophilia, fornication, drunkenness, drug abuse), but always keep the Law hovering over the sinner. Otherwise, you will just be seen as a "holier-than-thou" preacher. The Law will keep focus on the fact that it is *God* who is offended by sin, and it is God to whom we are all answerable. We can bring up the wickedness of abortion when we open up the Sixth Commandment. However, it is a very emotional subject (and so it should be), so don't get into a shouting match with an angry person. Say that it's murder, and the blood of the murdered child is on the hands of those who took its life, then move on. Remember, it is the Law that brings conviction of sin, so that's what we want to focus on.

3

Do you think it is best to have interaction with the audience or just do straightforward preaching?

Whether you are talking to 1 person, 2 people or 200, it is wonderful to have people ask questions. Just make sure you stay in control of the direction of the conversation. Don't get sidetracked, and don't get into arguments.

4

If you encounter people who are willing to talk but have lots of questions about Christianity, other religions and so on, how much time do you spend with them versus moving on to someone else who might be more "ripe for harvest," if you will? I don't mean people who are antagonistic; I mean people who have genuine concerns or issues that they've been struggling with.

People who keep asking questions don't see the urgency of the issue. There comes a point when you have to ask, "If you died right now, where would you go?" If the person is unsaved, you want him to give the right answer: "Hell." Then ask, "What are you going to do about it?" You want him to say that he will repent and trust the Savior. Then you ask, "When are you going to do that?" You want him to say, "Right now." If he hasn't come to that point, then you need to put the screws on. Take the person through the Law again and show him that he is a criminal who has been commanded by God Himself to repent and trust in the Savior. The time has come to stop the questions for the moment and do what He commands. Then, once he is right with God, he can look into those questions, if he still has them.

5

How do you deal with multiple objections from different people who come to you at almost the same time?

Whether you are preaching open-air or speaking to a small handful, you have to take control. Just say, "One at a time, please. Sir, please let the lady speak first." Speak with authority or you will have a circus on your hands.

6

How do you respond to someone who heads off your witnessing effort by quoting "judge not, lest ye be judged"?

Jesus told His disciples not to judge *each other*. That command doesn't mean that we are not to make moral judgments. He also tells us that when we judge, we should use "righteous judgment" (John 7:24). And isn't the person who's accusing you of being judgmental making a judgment about you? It's important to make it clear that whenever we speak about sin, we *are* making a moral judgment, but it is based on God's standards, not ours. The moral Law is the righteous standard by which all of us will be judged. So, helping people see how they'll do when they stand before God on Judgment Day isn't being judgmental—it's being compassionate.

7

When someone refuses to complete the good person test, how do you end the conversation on a good note? For example, if he or she says, "I don't want to continue this conversation," how do you respond?

That is difficult. It doesn't happen very often, but when it does, I say that I am sorry for offending them and that I hope they have a nice day. You never know what their experience may be. Perhaps they have had a friend who was pulled into a religious cult and they are paranoid of being deceived. Or maybe they have just lost a loved one and the pain is too much to take. The way you conclude the conversation may be a witness to them, so go out of your way to be kind, understanding, loving and gentle.

8

How important is it to know the verse references when witnessing?

It is important to know your way around the Bible; but with computers, you can find a Scripture in seconds. So don't fear that someone is going to ask, "Where is that in the Bible?" It rarely happens, and you can always say, "I will find out for you and let you know." The odds are that they don't really care.

9

What do you do when you're using the Law in a group situation and a Christian starts to diffuse the power of the Law by mentioning grace too soon?

I ask him to please wait and listen to what I am saying, and then share his thoughts in a few moments. That usually works.

10

What do you do when other Christians take away the seed that has been planted?

I seriously struggle to keep my cool. They will listen to me open up the Law, speak of Judgment Day and hell, and then say something like, "That doesn't sound very loving to me." When I hear that, I pray for special grace and turn my attention to them for a moment and question them in front of their friend or the crowd. It usually goes something like this: "Where will this man go if he dies in his sins?" The professing Christian usually says, "He will be separated from God." So I press him: "What is the name of the place where he will go to?" He will say, "To a terrible place."

I press him further as to what it's called. When I finally get him to say the word "hell," I say, "That's not very loving . . . or is it? If you believe he would go to hell for all eternity, do you warn him, or do you let him go there unwarned? If you care about this man, then let me talk to him about his salvation and you quietly pray that God helps me. Thanks." That approach usually works. I then approach him afterwards, shake his hand and give him a CD of "Hell's Best Kept Secret."

11

If you find yourself losing your patience, what do you do?

I remember once feeling very impatient with some hecklers. I could feel anger in my eyes, so I said to the crowd, "I'll be back in a few moments." I found somewhere quiet and asked God to forgive me for impatience. The break and the prayer did help.

12

How do you redeem yourself when you have done something wrong—sinned, become angry, misstated Scripture, let the crowd get out of hand, provoked a sinner to anger, given a "watered down" presentation of the gospel, and so forth?

You simply apologize where necessary. Ask God for forgiveness. Then learn from your mistakes. We all make them; so don't be discouraged. Don't allow mistakes to become stumbling blocks, rather let them be stepping-stones. Bruises give us memories to help us to avoid future pitfalls.

13

How do you avoid things that will tempt you and may even cause you to stumble as you go into the darkness?

I currently open-air preach at Huntington Beach in Southern California, where people wear "string" as an excuse for a bathing suit. If you find yourself in these situations, you have to let the fear of the Lord be your guide. Deal with it in prayer before you go, and if you stumble with your eyes, be very quick to repent. If it becomes a problem, avoid such places.

What if you are confronted with a serious personal situation with a stranger who requires immediate help? What do you do if you don't know what to do?

It sounds like you are concerned about "giants" in the land. I have never had that happen. So cast down your imaginations, and if by chance something like this does happen, God will give you the wisdom you need to handle it.

ENDING THE ENCOUNTER

No pursuit of mortal men is to be compared with that of soul winning.
CHARLES SPURGEON

1

Doesn't your teaching state that one shouldn't lead someone in a "sinner's prayer"?

I *do* believe in praying with sinners who come to Christ. The following is from *The Evidence Bible* (commended by Franklin Graham and Dr. James Kennedy):

To pray or not to pray? The question often arises about what a Christian should do if someone is repentant. Should we lead him in what's commonly called a "sinner's prayer" or simply instruct him to seek after God? Perhaps the answer comes by looking to the natural realm. As long as there are no complications when a child is born, all the doctor needs to do is *guide the head*. The same applies spiritually. When someone is "born of God," all we need to do is guide the head—make sure that they *understand* what they are doing. Philip the evangelist did this with the Ethiopian eunuch. He asked him, "Do you understand what you are reading?" (Acts 8:30). In the parable of the sower, the true convert (the "good soil" hearer) is he who hears "and understands." This understanding comes by the Law in the hand of the Spirit (Romans 7:7). If a sinner is ready for the Savior, it is because he has been drawn by the Holy Spirit (John 6:44). This is why we must be careful to allow the Holy Spirit to do His work and not rush in where angels fear to tread. Praying a "sinner's prayer" with someone who isn't genuinely repentant may leave you with a stillborn in your hands.

Therefore, rather than *lead* him in a prayer of repentance, it is wise to encourage him to pray himself. When Nathan confronted David about his sin, he didn't lead the king in a prayer of repentance. If a man committed adultery, and his wife is willing to take him back, should you have to write out an apology for him to read to her? No. Sorrow for his betrayal of her trust should spill from his lips. She doesn't want eloquent words, but simply sorrow of heart. The same applies to a prayer of repentance. The words aren't as important as the presence of "godly sorrow." The sinner should be told to repent—to confess and forsake his sins. He could do this as a whispered prayer, then you could pray for him. If he's not sure what to say, perhaps David's prayer of repentance (see Psalm 51) could be used as a model, but his own words are more desirable.

2

Are altar calls biblical? If they aren't, why are so many evangelical churches doing them?

The altar is mentioned often in the Scriptures, but there's no mention of an altar call. Then again, we don't know if the 3,000 who were saved on the day of Pentecost came forward to some sort of "altar" or place of prayer. The problem I have with modern-day altar calls isn't the call to come forward. The problem I have is with all the trimmings that come with it—music to stir the emotions, counselors coming forward to encourage a response (and to stop the preacher from looking stupid if there's no response). Add to that the fact that many altar calls aren't calling people to repentance, but to a happier lifestyle, and it's easy to see the damage that is being done to the cause of the gospel.

3

After leading people to Christ, how do you follow up with them? What tools do you give for them to develop their own personal relationship with Christ?

As I often say, our methodology will reflect our theology. I am convinced from Scripture that if someone truly comes to Christ, it is a work of God. And if he is "born of God," God will take care of him, with or without my follow up. Philip left the Ethiopian without follow up. God took Philip away from the man just after he professed faith and was baptized.

Nevertheless, I give any new converts our booklet called "Save Yourself Some Pain," which contains 10 principles for Christian growth. There they will find encouragement to read the Bible daily and obey it, share their faith and get into fellowship. However, a genuine convert will do these things anyway. They will love God's Word and feed on it; they will want to be with other Christians; and they cannot help but share their faith. Understanding true and false conversion means that we don't have to be a priest (a mediator) between the professed convert and God.

To help the person find a good church, you may want to get his contact details so you can send him information about the nearest church (your church or one in his community). Then ask the pastor of that fellowship to contact the person and extend a personal invitation to his church.

4

What is the difference between "follow up" and "discipleship"?

Follow up (in the modern sense) is when we get decisions, either through crusades or local church services, and we take laborers from the harvest field, who are few as it is, and give them this disheartening task of running after these "decisions" to make sure they're continuing with God. One just has to speak to any follow-up team to know how disheartening it can be to try to get unwilling "converts" to come to church when there is no Holy Spirit driving them to do so internally. There is actually a true incident of a new "convert" being found hiding in his closet when the follow-up person came to visit.

Again, if a person is soundly saved by the Holy Spirit, it's because he was drawn by the Holy Spirit and is now indwelt by the Holy Spirit. He will *want* to know more about God and will *seek* spiritual food. *I believe in feeding a new convert. I believe in nurturing him. I believe in discipling him—that's biblical and most necessary.* But I don't believe in following him. I can't find it in Scripture. I believe that when a person becomes a Christian, he becomes a disciple. When I bring a person to Christ through the power of the gospel, I make him a disciple. So when I preach the gospel to the unsaved and someone comes to Christ, I am "making disciples of all men."

It is common to believe that we are to get people saved and then make "disciples" of them. But if that's the case, we have a dilemma. Is the person not a "disciple" when he surrenders to Jesus? Is Jesus not his Lord? If he isn't discipled to Him, he's not a Christian. If he is saved, but he *becomes* a disciple at a certain point in his Christian walk, who decides that point?

So, to answer the question, follow up is running after a professed believer, while discipleship is living the normal Christian life. The message "True and False Conversion" explains this thoroughly. You can listen to it freely at www.livingwaters.com/learn/trueandfalse.htm.

5

Is there ever a time I can give someone assurance of salvation, or should I avoid it altogether?

Assurance in the believer is the job of the Holy Spirit (see Romans 8:16). However, you can point out assurance verses (such as Romans 10:9-10 or 1 John 5:11-13), and then tell the person to appropriate faith in them.

6

Why is it that you do not stress the importance of baptism? I won't add the many Scripture verses commanding baptism for the remission of our sins, because I am sure you already know them . . . just curious because I read it to be essential.

Water baptism is not essential to salvation. If you read Acts 10:44-48 carefully, you will see that the Gentiles received the Holy Spirit (they passed from death to life) before they were water baptized. Paul himself was filled with the Holy Spirit before he was baptized (see Acts 9:17-18). Also, the apostle Paul said that Christ sent him not to baptize, but to preach the gospel (see 1 Corinthians 1:17). It is the gospel that is the power of God to salvation, so that's what we preach. Nevertheless, it is important for the believer to obey the command to be baptized in water, which symbolically demonstrates identification with Christ in His death (under the water) and His resurrection (up out of the water). It is also a strong declaration to others of your faith in Christ alone for salvation.

GENERAL QUESTIONS ON DOCTRINE

*If you wish to know God, you must know His Word. If you wish to perceive
His power, you must see how He works by His Word. If you wish to know His purpose
before it comes to pass, you can only discover it by His Word.*
CHARLES SPURGEON

1

Why are there so many religions?

Mankind seems to mess up anything to which he puts his hand. He has excelled in the subject of religion. This is because idolatry knows no bounds. It's as far-reaching as the imagination of man. First, you create a god, and then you build a religion around it.

2

How do you respond to a person who says the Bible was written by a bunch of crazy people and you have to be crazy to believe it?

I would say, "Let's not argue about the inspiration of the Bible for a moment," and then I would take him through the Commandments. Jesus didn't say, "Go into all the world and convince people that the Bible is the Word of God." It is the *gospel* that is the power of God to salvation (see Romans 1:16), and the way to give the arrow of the gospel its thrust is to put it into the bow of the Law.

We often hear that Christianity stands or falls on the validity of Scripture. I respectfully disagree. I believe the Bible is God's Word. There's no argument there. But my salvation isn't dependent upon that fact, because I wasn't converted by a Bible. I was converted by the power of God, and when I picked up a Bible, it simply explained what had happened to me.

In our sincere efforts to convince a sinful world, we tend to use intellectual arguments (I'm often guilty of this) when the ultimate proof is the power of God transforming the human heart. But I didn't come to Christ through an intellectual argument, and my faith doesn't stand on human wisdom, so why should I try to bring others through that door?

If the whole scientific world came together and "disproved" the Bible, and archaeologists found what were "proved" to be the bones of Jesus, it wouldn't shake my faith in the slightest. Not at all. This is what Paul speaks about in 1 Corinthians 2:4-5 when he says that the Christian's faith doesn't rest "in the wisdom of men but in the power of God."

Remember, Early Christians weren't converted by the Scriptures. Instead, they were saved by a *spoken* message. The New Testament hadn't been compiled. There was no such thing as the printing press. And most couldn't read anyway.

If you believe that our foundation for the faith is the written Scriptures rather than in the person of Jesus Christ, I have some questions for you. When did Christianity begin? Was it on the Day of Pentecost when the 3,000 were converted by the power of God, or did it have to wait until the New Testament was compiled in 200 A.D.?

So don't feel that it's your mandate to convince anyone of the inspiration of the Word of God. You will never do it while they love their sins. For every reasonable argument you come up with, he will come back with a 101 atrocities and injustices in the Bible.

Instead, give the arrow of the gospel thrust by using the Law of God to bring the knowledge of sin. Make the sinner thirst after righteousness, without which he will perish. Then, once he is born again and comes to know the Lord, the Scriptures will open up to him. Until that time, the things of God will seem foolishness to him, as the Scriptures say (see 1 Corinthians 2:14).

3

I'm encountering more people who say, "Aren't morals simply the result of cultural upbringing and conditioning? We believe something is wrong just because everyone agrees it is wrong." How do you answer this?

This is called "moral relativism," and it's popular among those who don't realize there is such a thing as moral absolutes. The unchanging standard of morality is God's Law. God is perfect, holy, just and good, and so is His Law, because it issues from His very character. It is written in stone, and what's wrong for you is wrong for me and is wrong for every one of us. That's why it's essential to preach the Law of God. It is echoed by the conscience, and knowledge of it will cause the careless sinner to see his error.

If you ask a moral relativist if what Hitler did was *wrong*, he will say, "I would never do something like that myself, but I can't say it was *wrong*." He can't say that it was "wrong" because to him, nothing is *absolutely* right, and nothing is *absolutely* wrong. That has strong divine connotations.

So ask Mr. Relativist if pedophilia is wrong, and he will tell you that if it is against the law, it is simply wrong for *that* society. His framing of civil law is governed by whether or not people get "hurt," rather than by "right" or "wrong." His argument will be that pedophilia hurts children. But if someone takes pictures of naked children and posts them on the Internet without their knowledge (so that it's not hurting them), then it must be morally okay. So press him. Is pedophilia morally *wrong*? If he says that it's not, ask for his name and address, because you need to inform his neighbors and the local police that he is okay with pedophilia. If he admits that it's morally wrong *even though a society says that it's right*, then so was Hitler wrong, and there are, therefore, moral absolutes.

Be careful that you don't get mired in pseudo-intellectualism. It can be a time-waster, and you and I are told to redeem the time. You will simply win an argument, when what you should be doing is showing him that he needs God's forgiveness.

The root problem with a moral relativist is that his conscience is seared and, with the help of God, you *must* awaken it. So, say to him, "Let's just surmise that there is a heaven for a moment. Do you think you would be good enough to go there?" He will almost certainly say that he is (see Proverbs 20:6), so take him through the Good Person test. You are simply moving from the intellect (the place of argument), to the conscience (the place of the knowledge of right and wrong), so that it will do its God-given duty.

4

When it comes to lying, are there not conditions under which it is better to lie than to tell the truth, such as to protect someone's feelings? What about Rahab in Joshua 2? She lied to protect the spies, and they blessed her in return by sparing her family.

This is a contentious issue. Most husbands would lie if an armed burglar asked if his wife was hiding in the house. The reason he would lie is that if he said, "Yes, she's under the bed," then he is guilty of helping the burglar murder her. What would he say if he's forced at gunpoint to watch while the gunman rapes his wife before murdering her: "Sorry, honey; I didn't want to tell a lie"? These scenarios are often brought up by the unsaved to justify lying. But God knows the difference between incidents like these to protect the life of innocent victims, the use of "discretion" to protect someone's feelings, and bold, deceitful lies to protect ourselves.

5

Isn't it unreasonable that God would judge us by our thought life?

The idea that merely thinking could be a crime does seem absurd. That is, until you realize that if you merely conspire in your mind to kill the President of the United States, you will find yourself in serious violation of the law. Whether you express that thought verbally or in writing, you don't have to complete the act or even be actively planning it. You simply have to be thinking about it.

Some may say, "That's different. Conspiracy to murder the president is a serious crime." And that's the point. Most people don't think that sin against God is a serious crime. God does. Our moral standards are extremely low; God's are incredibly high. He is so holy that He requires perfection in thought, word and deed. If we have hatred in our heart for another person, God sees that as murder. And if we have lustful thoughts toward another human being, God sees that as committing adultery in our heart. He judges the thoughts and intent of our heart.

6

How do I know if I'm saved and simply caught up in a sinful habit or if I am not saved?

Every case is different. Many Christians have a sinful habit of overeating. Others may struggle with smoking or coveting. Others have a battle with sexual sins. The big question is do they stumble into sin or do they plan to sin? The Christian *falls* into sin; the false convert *dives* in. Some Christians believe in what is commonly called "sinless perfection" and think they can be completely without sin. I find that those folks usually have a problem with a subtle form of pride, which is a big sin.

So, none of us should look down on someone who is truly struggling with their sin. The key word is "struggling." If you are doing something that you know is wrong, don't make provision for the flesh. Avoid temptation. Don't go there. Feed yourself on the Word. Cultivate the fear of God in your life. Be busy sharing your faith. Continually pray for God's help. Have an accountability partner. Try not to be alone. Keep away from boredom, because the battleground is the mind. If you have a concern for the lost, the enemy is going to target your weakness, whatever it is. Be aware of that—that your battle isn't against flesh and blood, but against demonic forces. Resist them, steadfast in the faith.

7

If salvation is a free gift, why do we have to repent? It sounds as if we are paying for eternal life with our repentance.

Jesus paid the price for us, so there is nothing we can ever do ourselves to earn eternal life. It is a gift that God offers to us. In fact, we are so sinful and rebellious that both repentance and the faith that we exercise are given by God. Ephesians 2:8-9 tells us that faith is the gift of God, and 2 Timothy 2:24-25 says that repentance is "granted" to us by God. We can't even repent without God's help. Salvation is of the Lord—all of it, from beginning to end. He is the author and the finisher of our faith (see Hebrews 12:2). Just as our first birth was a gift from God to us, so is the second birth. This may raise questions about man's free will and God's sovereignty. Conquer any questions through trust.

8

When a person has accepted the Lord as his Savior but he or she walks away from God and back to the things of the world, can that person return to God and be forgiven?

When someone becomes a Christian, it is more biblical to say that he *surrendered* to God, rather than that he "accepted" Him. Those who merely "accept" Christ but don't surrender to His Lordship aren't truly born again and will fall away in time (see Luke 9:62). People in this category don't "return" to God because they never knew Him in the first place. I would suggest that you listen to the message "True and False Conversion" (www.livingwaters.com/learn/trueandfalse.htm).

9

What is the balance of assurance between salvation and examining yourself to see if you are in the faith?

Think of what you would do if you were wearing a parachute and waiting to jump out of a plane. You would have faith in the parachute, but you would also regularly check to make sure that the straps are firm. Once you have put on the Lord Jesus Christ through conversion (repentance and faith), you should regularly examine yourself to see how firm your relationship is with the Lord. Are you reading the Word daily? Do you have regular prayer? Are you fighting sin, or giving in to it? Are you living in holiness? Are you confessing sin? How is your relationship with other Christians? Is there any hidden bitterness against anyone? Are you sharing your faith? What is your greatest passion? Is it the Lord, or are material things more important? Do you love the world and the things in the world? On a scale of 1 to 10, how would you rate your walk with God? It should be a 10. If it's not, strive to make it a 10.

10

What does it mean to have the "righteousness of Christ"?

God accounts His own righteousness to us, so that we are not just prodigal sons who are forgiven but still smelling like a pigsty underneath. We are washed clean, clothed with a pure robe of righteousness and given a ring of inheritance.

11

The Bible seems to clearly say that God has predestined some people to heaven and some to hell. He has "chosen" or "elected" to save some and not others. All who are chosen are guaranteed to hear His voice and follow Him. Those who are not—well . . . they'll hear the Word but will never come to repentance. So, how do we reconcile these verses to the fact that God is "not willing that any should perish" (2 Peter 3:9)? Wouldn't He then have "called" everyone equally? Is there any earthly understanding to be found on this topic?

I normally keep silent about this issue, but you are so earnest that I wanted to share my thoughts. After more than 30 years of thinking about election and predestination, I find myself about where you are. I haven't figured it out, and I'm still working on it.

I know that God is sovereign. We don't do anything to be saved. We are saved by grace alone. But when I find myself leaning toward Calvinism, I think of a mass of verses that lean the other way. There are many Bible verses that say things to the effect that "whosoever will may come." Calvinists deal with them by adding a word here and there: "The Lord is not willing that any (of the elect) should perish but that all (of the elect) should come to repentance." "Whoever (of the elect) calls on the name of the Lord shall be saved." "God desires all men (who are the elect) to be saved and to come to the knowledge of the truth." That sends me back to the middle of the road.

Besides that, the issue is very divisive—a real church-splitter. So even if I did figure it out, I would keep it to myself for the sake of the ministry that God has entrusted me with. If I went one way or the other, doors would instantly slam.

So here is what I do to reconcile the issue in the privacy of my own mind: It's about 2000 B.C. You read in God's Word, "The earth hangeth upon nothing" (pre-*KJV*). You are instantly thrown into an intellectual dilemma. Science (and your own reason) tell you that can't be true. The earth is too heavy to "hang upon nothing." The law of gravity dictates that even a feather can't hang upon nothing.

So, you have to make a choice. Are you a "Bible-ite" or a "Reason-ite"? People are pressuring you to make a choice. What are you: Bible-ite or Reason-ite? But you don't have to go one way or the other. So you decide to stay in the middle, trusting God, and waiting about 4,000 years for some missing information.

It comes in A.D. 1800, when science discovers that there is no gravity in space. That missing information shows you how the earth (though it weighs multiple octillions of tons) can freely float in space, lighter than a feather.

So the question arises: What are you? Are you a Calvinist or are you an Arminian? You have to side with one or the other. Which camp are you in? Don't be a theological wimp. One way or the other. But you don't have to go one way or the other. Simply decide to stay in the middle, trusting God, and then patiently wait for some missing information.

The day will come when we will know all things (see 1 Corinthians 13:12), and when that time comes, and I suddenly understand how it was that two opposing thoughts could both be true, I will be glad that I didn't spend hours arguing with my brethren and causing division in the Body of Christ. It is then that I will be truly glad that I instead put my time and energy into reaching out to the lost.

(12)

Can you explain why Christians worship on Sunday instead of keeping the Sabbath?

We keep the first day of the week because that's what the disciples did. There is no command anywhere in the New Testament for Christians to keep the Jewish Sabbath. In fact, the Scriptures say we should not let any man tell us what day to keep. Seventh Day Adventists are welcome to keep the Sabbath, but they shouldn't attempt to tell others to do as they do. If they had half as much zeal for the lost as they do for telling Christians what day to rest, we would have revival.

(13)

In your analogy about pulling people into the lifeboat, perhaps not all of the people behind you are polishing brass. Some people (prayer support) are holding onto your belt to keep you from falling back into the icy water, and others (those who minister to new believers) are wrapping those icy victims in blankets, giving them soup, and so forth. Are the people doing the other jobs "not saved" because they aren't leaning out all the time and pulling people into the boat?

I appreciate what you are saying. But our problem is that 98 percent of the professed Body of Christ in America *are* praying and ministering to new believers. Only 2 percent are reaching out to the unsaved. So let's put it another way. Imagine that a number of little children sneak out of a house, get into a rubber raft in a swimming pool, and it overturns. Their parents hear them scream, rush outside and see that the kids are drowning. Each of the adults can swim, but instead of jumping in, they stand back and let one man try to save all the children.

At the court hearing on the deaths of five of the kids, the defense of those who stood back was that they saw their job as being one of getting warm towels and dry clothing ready for the children, for when they were rescued. The judge would be horrified at their defense and say that their *real* motive was that they did not want to get cold and wet. He would no doubt say that the blood of those dead children was on their guilty hands, and give each of them stiff prison terms.

Every Christian has been told to do more than stand back and pray. We have been *commanded* to jump into the waters of personal evangelism (see Matthew 28:19-20; Mark 16:15; 2 Corinthians 5:19-20). Yet most choose to do *everything but* what we have been commanded to do.

Personally, I would rather stand back and let other people reach out to the lost, but I can't. How could I say that the love of God dwells in me if I let people perish, simply because I was concerned about my own comfort and well-being? Love could never do that. If I stood back and busied myself with other things, I then could not have assurance (biblically) that I had passed from death to life. That's why Charles Spurgeon said, "Have you no wish for others to be saved? Then you are not saved yourself, be sure of that."

But the lack of laborers isn't the problem. That's just the symptom. The problem is that we have millions of false converts sitting in the Church. They have cold hearts and don't love their neighbor as much as they love themselves. But when someone is truly born again, the love of Christ "constrains" him. They immediately reach out to the unsaved. The will of God to seek the lost becomes their number-one priority. And how could it not, with so many perishing around us?

14

I love sharing the Lord with people and do so often, but I have learned that God has a specific place and function for me, and that is where I focus my energies. It seems you believe that if everyone is not out there doing "your method" of evangelism, then perhaps they are not even saved. All of us should be representatives of the Body and should always be prepared to witness where called to do so, but I think that some are to be planters and some should feed, and some are to harvest and some glean. Do you believe that if I am gleaning–picking up those who fall–that I am not doing what I am called to do?

The main parallel to the human body is in 1 Corinthians 12:14-31. Each part has its own function. That's a healthy body. But notice in that passage, the parallel is in-reach (within the local church), not outreach (evangelism): "And God has appointed these in the church: first apostles, second prophets, third teachers . . ." (v. 28). There is no mention of evangelists in that portion of Scripture because it's in the context of the Church coming together; and when all those functions are working well, we have a healthy Church. Then, when the Church is healthy, it will (as one Body) do what it has been commanded to do by the Head: to reach out to the lost.

We are like survivors in a lifeboat of the *Titanic*. All around us are drowning people. We need every hand onboard to help reach those who are drowning and pull them into the boat. We think and move as one mind and one body. Nothing else matters. Love is our motivation. Every hand is needed—because there is a terrible lack of rescuers. Why? Because some think that their job is to sit in the lifeboat and, knowing that people are perishing, busy themselves polishing the brass. If that's the case, one has to question if they are really part of the Body, because the Head has commanded us to reach out to those who are perishing (see Mark 16:15). A hand that doesn't do what the Head commands it to isn't healthy.

I'm not concerned what "method" people use to reach out, as long as they are doing it the way the Bible tells us to. Otherwise, they are just pulling corpses into the boat, and we see the fruit of that within the contemporary Church.

ADDITIONAL
MATERIALS

The following material contains review information on the quotes, useful Scriptures and quotes on witnessing, and practical tips for evangelism. They can be copied and given out to participants who are interested in learning more about sharing their faith.

REVIEW

This section will review much of what you've learned today. It would be wise for you to plan to read through it thoroughly tonight, and then again tomorrow to help you retain as much as possible from this training.

The Ten Commandments

Memorize the Ten Commandments if you haven't already. As the means of awakening the conscience of unbelievers, they are invaluable and should be committed to memory. The pictures below should help you.

"You shall have no other gods before Me"
(God should be #1 in your life)

"You shall not make for yourself a carved image"
(Don't bow down to anything but God)

"You shall not take the name of the LORD your God in vain"
(Don't use your lips to dishonor God)

"Remember the Sabbath day, to keep it holy"
(Don't neglect the things of God)

"Honor your father and your mother"
(Respect your parents)

"You shall not murder"
(Don't take the life of another)

"You shall not commit adultery"
(Adultery leaves a heart broken)

"You shall not steal"
(Don't take what is not yours)

"You shall not lie"
(Always speak the truth)

"You shall not covet"
(Don't want what others have)

© 2009 Kirk Cameron and Ray Comfort. Permission to photocopy granted.

Light to Dust

You've just dusted the table clean and pulled back the curtains to let in the early morning light. What do you see on the table? Dust. In the air? Dust. Did the light create the dust? No, it simply exposed the dust. In the same way, the light of God's Law shows us as we truly are, exposing the sin in our lives.

The "Good" News

If I were to approach you and tell you that someone you don't know just paid a $25,000 speeding ticket on your behalf, it wouldn't be "good" news to you, it would be foolishness—you would say, "I don't have a $25,000 speeding ticket"—and it would be offensive because I would be insinuating that you've broken the law when you don't think you have. However, suppose I were to tell you this: "On the way to this meeting, the law clocked you going 55 MPH through an area set aside for a blind children's convention, and there were 10 clear warning signs stating that 15 MPH was the limit, but you went straight through at 55 MPH. What you did was extremely dangerous. The law was about to take its course when someone you don't know stepped in and paid your fine for you. You are very fortunate." Can you see how telling you what you've done wrong first actually makes the good news make sense?

In the same way, when we approach unbelievers and tell them that Jesus died on the cross for their sins, it will be foolishness to them and offensive because as far as they're concerned, there are many people much worse than them. It would make sense, however, if we were to first bring instruction to them through the Law and allow the Divine Law to serve the purpose for which it was intended—to convert the soul (see Psalm 19:7). The good news of Christ's sacrifice will make sense after the Law acts as a mirror to the soul of unbelievers so that they see themselves in their sin as God does and realizes how it leaves them guilty before the judgment seat of God.

Improve Your Flight

Here is a story of two airplane passengers who were both told to wear a parachute, but for different reasons.

The first passenger was told to put the parachute on because it would improve his flight. He was skeptical at first, but he decided to give it a try and put the parachute on. Immediately, he felt its weight on his shoulders and how difficult it became to sit upright. The other passengers began to look at him and laugh, mocking him. At this, he pulled off the parachute and threw it to the ground in disgust. His heart was filled with bitterness toward those who gave him the parachute because as far as he's concerned, he was told an

© 2009 Kirk Cameron and Ray Comfort. Permission to photocopy granted.

outright lie. It will be a long time before anyone gets one of those things on his back again.

The second passenger was told to put the parachute on because at any moment during the flight he would have to jump out of the plane at 25,000 feet. He gladly put the parachute on, not noticing its weight on his shoulders or the other passengers mocking him. His mind was consumed with the thought of what would happen to him if he were to jump without that parachute.

In the same way, if we were to approach unbelievers and say that they needed to accept Jesus Christ as their Lord and Savior and that if they did they would receive love, joy, peace and lasting happiness, they would come for the wrong motive. They would likely fall away, being likened as a stony ground hearer—receiving the Word with joy and gladness but not having roots enough to stand. They would put on the Savior in an experimental manner to see if the claims were true. Then, when the promised persecution and tribulation came, they would likely fall away. In essence, we have told these unbelievers that Jesus would improve their flight, and when the flight got bumpy they would become bitter, cast off the Savior and resent those who had told them this "good news."

However, if we were to first bring instruction, through the Law, of how they have transgressed the Law and sinned against God (see 1 John 3:4), allowing the Law to reveal how God looks on sin, they will come to the Lord in true repentance and will have "all joy and peace in believing" (Romans 15:13). Then, when the flight got bumpy, they would not cast off the Savior—they didn't come for a better flight; they came to be saved from the wrath to come! In fact, tribulation would drive true believers closer to the Father, as they clung tightly to the Savior and even looked forward to the jump.

Law to the Proud and Grace to the Humble

Biblical evangelism has always been Law to the proud and grace to the humble. With the Law, God breaks the hard heart, and with the gospel, He heals the broken heart. Never will you see Jesus giving the gospel to a proud, arrogant man, because He always did those things that please the Father. God resists the proud and gives grace to the humble (see James 4:6), so don't feel pressured to give the good news to proud, self-righteous sinners. Once the Law has humbled them, they will be ready for grace. Here are two examples of Law to the proud:

- **Luke 10:25-37: Professing expert on God's Law tested Jesus.** Jesus pointed this expert to the Law because he was a proud, arrogant, self-righteous man who was not seeking the truth but was in essence saying, "And what do You think I must do to inherit eternal life?" Jesus gave him the Law, and when he wanted to justify

© 2009 Kirk Cameron and Ray Comfort. Permission to photocopy granted.

himself by asking who was his "neighbor," Jesus told him the parable of the "good" Samaritan who simply obeyed the most basic of the commandments—loving his neighbor as himself.

- **Luke 18:18-25: Rich young ruler wants eternal life.** Jesus gave him five horizontal commandments relating to man, and when he said he had kept these since his youth, Jesus told him he lacked one thing. Jesus knew this man's god was his money. When He told him to sell all he had, distribute it to the poor, and follow Him, the man went away very sorrowful because he loved his money more than God.

Here are two examples of grace to the humble:

- **John 3:1-21: Nicodemus.** Nicodemus humbly came to Jesus recognizing the deity of Christ.

- **Acts 2: Jews on the day of Pentecost.** These "devout Jews" were humble of heart, there to celebrate the giving of God's Law on Mt. Sinai.

Scripture Explaining the Functions of God's Law

Psalm 19:7: "The law of the LORD is perfect, converting the soul."

Romans 2:15: "Who show the work of the law written in their hearts, their conscience also bearing witness" [con = "with"; science = "knowledge"].

Romans 3:19: "Now we know that whatever the law says, it says to those who are under the law, that every mouth may be stopped, and all the world may become guilty before God."

Romans 3:20: "Therefore by the deeds of the law no flesh will be justified in His sight, for by the law is the knowledge of sin."

Romans 7:7: "What shall we say then? Is the law sin? Certainly not! On the contrary, I would not have known sin except through the law."

2 Corinthians 7:10: "For godly sorrow produces repentance to salvation."

Galatians 3:11: "But that no one is justified by the law in the sight of God is evident, for 'the just shall live by faith.'"

© 2009 Kirk Cameron and Ray Comfort. Permission to photocopy granted.

Galatians 3:24: "Therefore the law was our tutor to bring us to Christ, that we might be justified by faith."

1 Timothy 1:8-9: "But we know that the law is good if one uses it lawfully [for the purpose for which it was designed], knowing this: that the law is not made for a righteous person, but for the lawless and insubordinate, for the ungodly and for sinners."

Hebrews 9:27: "And as it is appointed to men to die once, but after this the judgment."

Hebrews 10:16-17: "This is the covenant that I will make with them after those days, said the Lord: I will put My laws into their hearts, and in their minds I will write them . . . their sins and their lawless deeds I will remember no more."

James 2:10: "For whoever shall keep the whole law, and yet stumble in one point, he is guilty of all."

1 John 3:4: "Whosoever committeth sin transgresseth also the law: for sin is the transgression of the law" (*KJV*).

Quotes on the Use of the Law in Witnessing

Oswald Chambers: "Conscience is the internal perception of God's Moral Law."

A.B. Earl: "I have found by long experience that the severest threatenings of the Law of God have a prominent place in leading men to Christ. They must see themselves as lost before they will cry for mercy; they will not escape danger until they see it."

Billy Graham: "The Holy Spirit convicts us . . . He shows us the Ten Commandments; the Law is the schoolmaster that leads us to Christ. We look at the mirror of the Ten Commandments, and we see ourselves in that mirror."

Matthew Henry: "Of this excellent use is the Law: it converts the soul, opens the eyes, prepares the way of the Lord in the desert, rends the rocks, levels the mountains, makes a people prepared for the Lord."

Martin Luther: "The proper effect of the Law is to lead us out of our tents and tabernacles, that is to say, from the quietness and security wherein we dwell, and from trusting in ourselves, and to bring us before the presence of God, to reveal His wrath to us, and to set us before our sins."

© 2009 Kirk Cameron and Ray Comfort. Permission to photocopy granted.

Martin Luther: "The first duty of the gospel preacher is to declare God's Law and show the nature of sin."

Charles Spurgeon: "No pursuit of mortal men is to be compared with that of soul winning."

Charles Spurgeon: "The conscience of a man, when he is really quickened and awakened by the Holy Spirit, speaks the truth. It rings the great alarm bell. And if he turns over in his bed, that great alarm bell rings out again and again, 'The wrath to come! The wrath to come!'"

Charles Spurgeon: "They will never accept grace until they tremble before a just and Holy Law."

John Wesley: "Before I can preach love, mercy, and grace, I must preach sin, Law, and judgment."

John Wesley: "It is the ordinary method of the Spirit of God to convict sinners by the Law. It is this which, being set home in the conscience, generally breaketh the rocks in pieces. It is more especially this part of the Word of God, which is quick and powerful, full of life and energy and sharper than any two-edged sword."

© 2009 Kirk Cameron and Ray Comfort. Permission to photocopy granted.

QUICK REFERENCE CARD

You can cut this out, fold it in half, and laminate it. Or, a laminated color version of this Quick Reference Card is also available for purchase from www.WayoftheMaster.com. You can easily fit it in your pocket or purse to serve as a quick reference you can glance at before witnessing to someone.

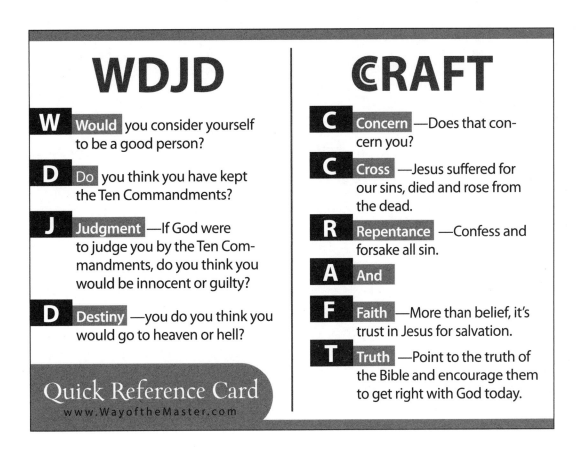

WDJD

W Would you consider yourself to be a good person?

D Do you think you have kept the Ten Commandments?

J Judgment —If God were to judge you by the Ten Commandments, do you think you would be innocent or guilty?

D Destiny —you do you think you would go to heaven or hell?

Quick Reference Card
www.WayoftheMaster.com

CRAFT

C Concern —Does that concern you?

C Cross —Jesus suffered for our sins, died and rose from the dead.

R Repentance —Confess and forsake all sin.

A And

F Faith —More than belief, it's trust in Jesus for salvation.

T Truth —Point to the truth of the Bible and encourage them to get right with God today.

© 2009 Kirk Cameron and Ray Comfort. Permission to photocopy granted.

KNOCK, KNOCK!

A FEW PRACTICAL TIPS ON SHARING YOUR FAITH

BY EMEAL ("E.Z.") ZWAYNE

Emeal ("E. Z.") Zwayne is the executive vice president of Living Waters Publications.
Make sure you listen to his "Passing the Torch" CD (which has been referred to as a life-changing teaching)
available through www.livingwaters.com (click on the "store" link and then the "audio" link).

Now that you have finished the *Conquer Your Fear, Share Your Faith* course, you understand that each of us has been commanded to go into all the world and share the gospel. But how exactly do we accomplish this? One approach is door-to-door evangelism—but it can be extremely nerve-racking. Just the thought of walking up to a stranger's door to share the gospel is enough to send the bravest of us into a severe panic attack, or at least hyperventilation. However, for those who are so inclined, this is a wonderful opportunity to present the soul-saving gospel of our Savior. If you're willing to be used by the Lord in this way, I've provided a few tips to help you in the process.

Round Up Helpers

When going door-to-door, a great way to get people's attention is to begin by offering to do small handyman chores for free. This gesture is an effective way to demonstrate your care and concern for your neighbors.

To round up the necessary helpers, first put out two sign-up sheets at your church and make an announcement to the congregation. Explain that you are seeking people who are interested in using their handyman skills to freely serve the community when called on during an occasional weekend. Emphasize that their participation will be minimal and rarely

© 2009 Kirk Cameron and Ray Comfort. Permission to photocopy granted.

required (we have found that while most people sincerely appreciate the gesture to serve them, very few will ever call to request assistance). Also state that you are looking for people who are interested in witnessing door to door.

Once you have a reasonable number of people signed up (5 to 10, depending on your church size), specify a regular time and place that the witnessing team will meet each week (or however often you decide to go out).

Make a Plan

You will then need to map out the homes in your community. It's good to be systematic about your approach and keep records of every address, jotting down the names of people you speak with and the responses you receive. This will come in handy for future visitations. If your church doesn't have brochures or calling cards, don't forget to print up some cards containing the church contact information, address and other necessary information so that people can respond to your offer.

After assembling your teams, mapping out the homes in your community and gathering the necessary materials (including the questionnaire—see below), you are ready to begin. Always be sure to send people out in teams of two—no less (for their safety), and preferably no more (you don't want to intimidate people by appearing in a gang at their door!).

Prepare a Conversation-Starter

When you approach each door, you will need to have an idea of how you will begin the conversation. I recommend that you begin by saying something to this effect:

Hi, how are you today? I'm sorry to bother you at your home. I'll make this really quick. My name is _____ and this is my friend, _____. We're from _____, a local Christian church. We're not here to sell you anything or to get you to come to our church. We just wanted to let you know that we have a ministry set up to freely serve the community.

So, if you are ever doing any handyman work around your home—like painting, major gardening, putting up a fence—we have a team of people from our church who are eager to come out and help you. There is no charge, and absolutely no donations are accepted. And let me assure you that there are no strings attached. We just want to be a blessing to you. Here is a card with our contact information. Please don't ever hesitate to call us. It would be our pleasure to serve you in any way we can.

© 2009 Kirk Cameron and Ray Comfort. Permission to photocopy granted.

We're also conducting a quick questionnaire today. It's only three short questions and will take only two to three minutes. Would that be okay?

Conduct a Questionnaire

At this point, most people will be overwhelmed and blessed by your offer to freely serve them and open to participate in the questionnaire. The questionnaire should contain the following questions:

1. Do you believe in the existence of any type of god or higher power?

2. I'm sure you've heard of something called "Judgment Day." This is said to be the day when everyone will be judged by God and receive either heaven or hell for all eternity. If there truly was a coming Day of Judgment, do you think it would be important for people to know what they would need to do in order to go to heaven and avoid hell?

3. Because you believe this to be important [or, if they do not think it is important, say, "If you happen to be wrong and there is indeed a coming Judgment Day . . ."], do you think you would know what a person would need to do in order to go to heaven and avoid hell? If so, what would you say that is?"

You should summarize these questions on a printed questionnaire; however, it's important for members of the witnessing team to memorize these questions if possible rather than read them. They should glance down at the questionnaire only for a second, just to remember the gist of each question, and then look the person in the eye when communicating.

On the questionnaire, place two columns beside each question where the team member can mark a yes or no. It's not necessary to write down the person's answer about how someone can go to heaven and avoid hell. If anyone asks why you're conducting the questionnaire, the honest answer should be: "We are conducting this questionnaire to familiarize ourselves with the overall spiritual perspective of our community."

Ask Follow-up Questions

Once the questions have been asked, most people will begin to open up and share their opinions. It is very important that you listen attentively and closely at this point.

After they have finished sharing, transition by saying something such as, "Thank you so much. That concludes the questionnaire, but I have a couple of quick additional questions

© 2009 Kirk Cameron and Ray Comfort. Permission to photocopy granted.

to ask you on a personal level. Would you consider yourself to be an open-minded person?" Let the person respond. Then ask, "Do you respect other people's beliefs?"

The overwhelming majority of people will answer yes to these two questions. From that point, you can springboard into the gospel by saying, "I'm glad to hear that. Before we go, let me quickly tell you what we believe about the coming Day of Judgment and what you can do to go to heaven and avoid hell, since this is the most important matter in the world."

During the conversation, you can refer back to the fact that the person said he or she was open-minded and respectful of other people's beliefs in order to reinforce what you are saying. We've found this to be quite effective.

My team and I have used this approach at approximately 1,000 homes and with countless people throughout the years on the street and in public places. By God's grace, it has been a fruitful approach and has enabled us to share the gospel of salvation with many unsaved people.

While this is a good and proven format, remember that it is important to be flexible regarding the actual words that are used. This is simply meant to be a helpful guideline, so be sure to use the words with which you are most comfortable.

May the Lord bless you as you go, and may He open doors that no man can shut.

© 2009 Kirk Cameron and Ray Comfort. Permission to photocopy granted.

FISHING TIPS

Following are some additional details on how to have effective fishing trips that are a blessing to you and those you speak with.

Scout Your Local Fishing Hole

Drive around your city and look for places where people are milling about. You don't want a place where people are rushing from one place to another—you can't carry on a casual conversation with someone who's trying to get somewhere in a hurry.

Malls, flea markets, parks, beaches, perhaps even the front area of your local movie theater—these are all places where you will likely be able to find people who are not in any rush and are therefore more likely to talk to you.

Try to note the days of the week and times when there are lots of people present. Evenings and weekends are probably going to be your best times to find lots of people either window shopping or just waiting around.

Pick a Day and Time

With the information you collected about the best times and days to find lots of people at the fishing hole, talk to other interested fishermen to set a day and time you can all agree on to go out together. It's a good idea to make a commitment to fish there on a weekly basis. The advantage of making it a regular event is that people who want to join you from week to week will always know where to find you.

Select the Right Fishing Clothes

We usually do not encourage people to wear T-shirts with Christian sayings or slogans on them. A T-shirt that "shouts" may have the effect of scaring the fish away before you even get to open your mouth. Your team may come to another conclusion on this issue, but no matter what you decide to wear, everyone needs to be sure that their clothing is in keeping with Christian modesty.

Get Some Fishing Buddies

Whenever possible, those who are new and nervous should be paired with those who are more experienced. The more experienced person can do the talking for the first several times, and then begin encouraging the new fisher to take the lead. It's comforting for new fishers to have an "old pro" standing by in case they feel like they're suddenly in over their head.

Practice Casting

You can't catch any fish unless you can cast. A friendly smile and a courteous greeting are often all you need to start a conversation. Teach your team members to practice greeting strangers everywhere they go. Tell them to begin looking strangers in the eye, smiling and saying a simple, "Hello." For many people, this can be a very difficult step. However, if they begin to just practice being friendly, it will get easier over time.

Pack Your Tackle Box

Every good fisher needs some fishing "tackle." By this we mean that you need a way to break the ice with strangers. One of the best pieces of "tackle" is a unique gospel tract. Gospel tracts that are truly unique can be used to quickly and easily break the ice with strangers, while also swinging the conversation to the spiritual. Living Waters has tracts so unusual that unbelievers will chase you down asking for more—really.

It's also a great idea if you can learn a little sleight-of-hand. Simple tricks are great for breaking the ice with strangers (Ray also carries several silly pictures—see www.livingwaters.com/icebreakers.html—in his wallet for the same purpose). If you have a graphic program on your computer, you may be able to create your own silly pictures.

Reel in When You Get a Nibble

When talking to someone who seems sincere, we like to give out copies of "Save Yourself Some Pain." It contains a review of the gospel, as well as 10 steps for new and growing Christians. It's also a good practice to keep several New Testaments in your car. If you find out the person doesn't have a Bible, you can easily walk out to the parking lot to get one.

The question often arises about what a Christian should do if someone is repentant. Should we lead him in what's commonly called a "sinner's prayer" or simply instruct him to seek after God? Perhaps the answer comes by looking to the natural realm.

As long as there are no complications when a child is being born, all the doctor needs to do is guide the infant's head. The same applies spiritually. When someone is "born of God," all we need to do is guide the head—make sure that the person understands what he or she is doing. Philip the evangelist did this with the Ethiopian eunuch who was reading Scripture. He asked him, "Do you understand what you are reading?" (Acts 8:30). In the Parable of the Sower, the true convert (the "good soil" hearer) is he who hears "and understands" (see Matthew 13:23). This understanding comes by the Law in the hand of the Spirit (see Romans 7:7). If a sinner is ready for the Savior, it is because the Holy Spirit drew him (see John 6:44). This is why we must be careful to allow the Holy Spirit to do His work and not rush in where angels fear to tread.

Praying a sinner's prayer with someone who isn't genuinely repentant may leave you with a stillborn in your hands. Therefore, rather than lead him in a prayer of repentance, it is wise to encourage him to pray for himself. When Nathan confronted David about his sin, he didn't lead the king in a prayer of repentance.

If a man commits adultery, and his wife is willing to take him back, should you have to write out an apology for him to read to her? No. Sorrow for his betrayal of her trust should spill from his lips. She doesn't want eloquent words; she simply wants to hear sorrow of heart. The same applies to a prayer of repentance. The words aren't as important as the presence of "godly sorrow." The sinner should be told to repent—to confess and forsake his sins. He should first do this as a whispered prayer, and then you could pray for him. If he's not sure what to say, perhaps David's prayer of repentance (see Psalm 51) could be used as a model; but his own words are more desirable.

CLOSING THOUGHTS

God bless you for your concern for the lost, and for your concern that we reach out to them biblically. Never lose sight of what God is using you for. He has trusted you with the message of *everlasting life*. Never forget that you have an enemy, and perhaps his greatest weapon is discouragement. If you want to reach the lost and you particularly want to preach open-air, be ready for attacks. Be ready for fear. Be ready for discouragement to come from the least expected places. It will often come from Christian friends or family who will tell you that you are unloving or overboard. Being shot by your own side is called "friendly fire," but there's nothing "friendly" about it. It's worse than being shot from in front. So keep your shield of faith held high. Make sure you are soaked in the love of God. Be resolute. Be faithful.

Here's a prayer of resolution: *"Father, I thank you for the shed blood of Jesus. It is because of His blood that I can boldly come before Your throne. Please help me to always remember that You have trusted me with the message of salvation for this lost and dying world. Let Your love be my motivation. Help me never to be discouraged, distracted or disillusioned. Help me to keep my heart free from sin, and to always keep my eyes on Jesus, the author and finisher of our faith. Help me to always speak and preach, knowing that You are listening to my every word, and may I always be a true and faithful witness. In Jesus' precious name I pray. Amen."*

FOR FURTHER STUDY

Basic Training Course

This eight-session DVD course will teach you to simply and confidently share the gospel with family, friends and strangers by using a proven and powerfully effective way to present the gospel. Learn the forgotten biblical principle of bypassing the intellect (the place of argument) and speaking directly to the conscience (the place of the knowledge of right and wrong)—the way Jesus did. Lessons include overcoming fear, using tracts effectively, answering the top 10 questions, and more; and they contain fascinating on-the-street conversations. Weekly homework assignments will gradually coax you, step-by-step, out of your comfort zone to reach your loved ones for Christ. You will be inspired and motivated as you learn, watch and then do.

Intermediate Training Course

This eight-session DVD course adds critical framework to your foundation. It will teach you how to avoid the devastating pitfalls of producing false conversions. You will learn how to prove the existence of hell, both through the Scriptures and through reason, and what to do when things go wrong. Discover how to witness to a family member; how to witness to someone who is gay; how to recognize subtle satanic doctrines; how to refute the theory of evolution (join Kirk and Ray as they take an orangutan to lunch); and how to prove the existence of God.

School of Biblical Evangelism

With 101 lessons on subjects ranging from basic Christian doctrine to knowing your enemy; from false conversions to proving the deity of Jesus, you will be well equipped to answer questions as you witness to anyone. This study course will help you prove the authenticity of the Bible, provide ample evidence for creation, refute the claims of evolution, understand the beliefs of those in cults and other religions and know how to reach both friends and strangers with the gospel.

Join online at www.biblicalevangelism.com
or call 800-437-1893
to obtain the entire course in book form

ALSO AVAILABLE FROM
KIRK CAMERON &
RAY COMFORT

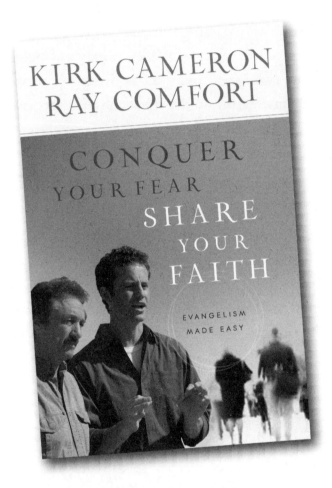

**CONQUER YOUR FEAR,
SHARE YOUR FAITH**
Kirk Cameron and Ray Comfort
ISBN 978.08307.51549
ISBN 08307.51548

As Christians, most of us realize that it is our responsibility to follow Jesus' command to go into all the world and preach the gospel to everyone. But for many of us, that is a terrifying thought. How can we approach complete strangers and start talking with them about Christ? In *Conquer Your Fear, Share Your Faith*, Kirk Cameron and Ray Comfort show how anyone can follow "the Way of the Master," the evangelism approach that Jesus used to overcome objections and help people realize their guilty state before God. They explain how you can approach friends, family, intellectuals or even atheists to strike up a meaningful conversation and have a discussion about that person's eternal destination. All it takes is overcoming your fear and taking that first step of faith.

Available at Bookstores Everywhere!
Visit **www.regalbooks.com** to join **Regal's FREE** e-newsletter. You'll get useful **excerpts** from our newest releases and **special access to online chats** with your favorite authors. Sign up today!

Regal
God's Word for Your World™
www.regalbooks.com